CHURCHILL, FRANCO AND THE SPANISH CIVIL WAR

Dedication

For Keir.
This book is also dedicated to the men and women who travelled to Spain in the 1930s to fight fascism.

It was not fraud or foolishness,
Glory, revenge, or pay:
We came because our open eyes
Could see no other way.

Cecil Day Lewis

CHURCHILL, FRANCO AND THE SPANISH CIVIL WAR

FRANK HOTCHKISS

Published by
Carn Publishing Ltd.
Lochnoran House,
Auchinleck,
Ayrshire,
KA18 3JW.

© Frank Hotchkiss 2024

First Published in 2024

ISBN - 978 1 911043 26 3

Printed in Great Britain by
Bell & Bain Ltd.
Glasgow, G46 7UQ.

The right of the author to be identified as the author of this work has been asserted by him in accordance with the Copyright, Designs and Patents Act 1988.
All rights reserved. No part of this publication may be reproduced, stored, or transmitted in any form, or by any means, electronic, mechanical or photocopying, recording or other-wise, without the express written permission of the publisher.

CONTENTS

Acknowledgements 6
About the author 6
Introduction 7
1: The 1920s: The rat and the King's dictator in pursuit
    of fool's gold 13
2: Changing of the guard, Britain and Spain 1930 – 1931 25
3: Looking left when the danger was from the right: Churchill in the wilderness and the Second Republic at "peace" 37
4: The calm before the storm 47
5: The election of the Popular Front, the German threat and
    the plotting of the Generals 57
6: The blondes in the Dragon Rapide 67
7: Position No. 1: Churchill backs the Nationalists 77
8: Family ties 89
9: Position No. 2: Non-intervention 99
10: Italy at war with the Spanish Republic and the flight
    of the Condor 109
11: Position No. 3: "The supreme farce of our time" 119
12: Soviet Union aid - a help and a hinderance 131
13: The International Brigades 141
14: End of the Civil War and Position No. 4: too little,
    too late 153
15: WWII – Churchill bribes Franco's Generals 165
16: Franco and Hitler 177
17: Gibraltar, Operation Pilgrim and Operation Mincemeat . . .187
Epilogue: Victory in 1945 and the defeat of the dictators*
    (*except in Spain) 197
References 203
Index 206

ACKNOWLEDGEMENTS

The author would like to thank several people who have influenced this book. The historians he has worked with, especially Hugh Hood and Robert Williamson, whose worlds collide in this work. Linda Semple, for reading the first version and for her kind words of support. Dane Love, for his invaluable advice and help in bringing this book to publication. All of the family and friends who have encouraged and put up with hearing about this book during its long gestation.

ABOUT THE AUTHOR

Frank Hotchkiss is the Director of Studies at Scottish Highers Online. During a varied career, he has been involved in education for over twenty years and although semi-retired, he still writes question papers for history and sociology exams as well as teaching online. Frank has written articles and plays previously, however this is his first book. Brought up in Clydebank, Frank now lives in West Kilbride in Ayrshire and can be contacted at: frankhotchkissauthor@gmail.com

The front cover shows the painting "Guernica" by Pablo Picasso. It depicts the devastation of the historic market town of that name by German bombers operating as part of Franco's Nationalist forces during the Spanish Civil War. Image: colaimages/Alamy Stock Photo.

INTRODUCTION

The first time that Winston Churchill saw military action, was on the side of the Spanish. As a young cavalry officer, who had ridden in the colours no further than Sandhurst and Aldershot, he volunteered, via connections of his late father and with funding from his mother, to join the Spanish forces in Cuba in 1895. At that time Spain was attempting to put down a rebellion by the island's population who were seeking independence (they would gain this in 1898). Churchill travelled with a fellow officer for some adventure and to try to witness combat for the first time. He also had a secret mission, from the British military, to report on the performance of a new type of bullet the Spanish were using. To part finance the trip, Churchill became a war correspondent for the *Daily Graphic*. During his short time at the front line (less than three weeks) he came under fire and won a medal, his first, although it was largely a courtesy rather than for anything he had done. Privately, Churchill expressed some sympathy for the rebels but in reality, he was on the side of the Imperialists, as he would be his entire life. The protection of the British Empire and a hatred of left-wing ideology were to be the two great guiding principles of his political beliefs, to the point of obscuring the truth from him on numerous occasions.

Churchill was a member of a prominent family in the British aristocracy, born in the family home of Blenheim Palace (his grandfather was the Duke of Marlborough) on 30th November 1874. Winston Churchill had no title but a great sense of entitlement. His father was Lord Randolf Churchill, a prominent politician whose meteoric rise saw him become Chancellor of the Exchequer at the age of 37. Lord Randolf resigned from the cabinet, having not completed a full six months in number 11 Downing Street, over the issue of defence spending, which he wished to cut. Even as a child, Winston could sense the disappointment in his household at a political career which had effectively ended. The young Winston idolised his father and was determined to follow in his footsteps, partly at least to rehabilitate the memory of the man. Forty years later, as Chancellor, Winston Churchill was greatly criticised for cuts to defence spending. When first appointed to the post he remarked that he still had his father's ceremonial robes of office.

A few days after Churchill was marking his 21st birthday in Cuba, Francisco Franco Bahamonde celebrated his third. Born in El Ferrol, a small naval town in Galicia in the extreme Northwest of Spain to a family of naval administrators, Franco was a second son whose childhood was blighted by the frequent absences of his philandering father, in a similar way that Churchill's was by the absences (physical and emotional) of both his father and mother. Franco's reaction was to attach himself to his mother and adopt her pious, religious nature and abhor his father's perceived liberalism and flirtations with freemasonry, which Franco was to grow to loathe. Franco's early days were blighted by the personal disruption caused by his parents' separation and the aftermath of the national humiliation following the loss of Cuba and the other colonies in 1898. Determined to join the navy, as was his family's tradition, Franco's education was at a naval preparatory school. His ambitions were thwarted by a change in policy that restricted entry (there was understandably much less need for a large Spanish navy now) but he was determined to pursue a military career. At the age of 14, Franco entered the military academy at Toledo to train as an officer in the army, a move which was eventually to have devastating consequences for Spain.

Spain was ruled in the early part of the 20th century by King Alfonso XIII who received the crown at birth since his father had died, aged just 27, before Alfonso was born. There was a parliament, the Cortes, but elections to it were largely rigged and the two main parties took turns to govern, so much so that the system was called the *Turno-pacifico* (peaceful turnaround) and occasionally results were published before the election had taken place. Understandably there was growing disquiet among sections of the Spanish people at this sham of democracy. Many of the Spanish bourgeoisie were frustrated by the prominence in decision-making of the land-owning aristocracy and wished to see a government which was more pro-business. Groups of workers and peasants, increasingly organised in socialist or anarchist trade unions, wanted more wholesale changes; and many of the intelligentsia railed against the strong influence of the Church and became vehemently anti-clerical. The King was clearly both unwilling and unable to effect change. The target of several assassination attempts, including one on his wedding day which killed 30 people and wounded 100 more, Alfonso seemed like a relic of the imperial Spain which no longer existed. Alfonso saw himself as a sportsman and head of the military. He lived the life of an idle playboy, with several mistresses and half a dozen illegitimate children. Ruling Spain was a hobby that was his alone to enjoy.

Churchill had been a Conservative MP from 1900 but crossed the floor in 1904 to join the Liberals. This was done largely over the issue of protectionism and tariff reform but also because Churchill recognised that the next election was likely to produce a Liberal landslide. Churchill became Liberal Home Secretary in 1910 and was responsible for events which dogged his political reputation for years – and in some cases, for ever. In particular, his use of metropolitan police in south Wales against striking miners and the deployment of soldiers to support the police, led to Churchill becoming a figure of hate among working class communities in south Wales and particularly Tonypandy. Although almost all of his biographers believe that Churchill's reputation has been ill-served by the folklore of these events, the criticisms are not completely without foundation. Mining communities affected knew that it was on Churchill's orders that London police and Lancashire troops were there to violently drive back the strikers. Much has been made of Churchill's "leniency" in not wanting the troops to open fire on the strikers and their families but although there were no shots, bayonets were used by the soldiers. Churchill had also been President of the Board of Trade and moved from the Home Office to be First Lord of the Admiralty, a post which he held in the First World War, with disastrous consequences. The fiasco of the Dardanelles campaign and the slaughter at Gallipoli, were events for which Churchill was chiefly responsible and led to him losing the Admiralty job which he so enjoyed.

In the spring of 1914, prior to the outbreak of the first World War, Churchill had visited Spain to play polo and whilst there, met King Alfonso XIII. The King presented him with his medal for serving (albeit extremely briefly) in Cuba nearly 20 years previously. Churchill met Alfonso several other times when the Spanish King came to Britain. Churchill was always deferential in the extreme towards royalty and this came to the fore when writing later about Alfonso, who he believed had given "faithful service to his country… governed always by love and respect for his people."[1] Churchill continued to fete Alfonso, (even after the part played by the King in assisting dictatorships in Spain in the 1920s) and this adherence to the traditional, anti-democratic strand of Spanish politics influenced Churchill's thoughts and actions when choosing sides at the outbreak of the Spanish Civil War.

The exploits of Franco and his fellow Generals in the 1930s and the reactions of Churchill to the plight of Spain, were founded in their early days. They were men who sought adventure and advancement when they were young; and both did

---
1 Winston Churchill, *Great Contemporaries*, p 159.

INTRODUCTION

so successfully, long before the events which were to make them famous later in their lives as leaders of their countries. Their attitudes to the tragedy of Spain in the 1930s were also shaped by their core beliefs. They shared an abhorrence of communism and any similar ideologies. They had a heightened sense of nationalism: for Franco, the *Patria* was above all; for Churchill it was the British Empire. To understand how Churchill, a man remembered as an arch anti-appeaser and the scourge of despots, came to support a dictator who destroyed a European democracy and found himself on the same side as Nazi Germany and fascist Italy, one must appreciate his motivations throughout his long political career. Churchill and Franco were both products of their time and class, but to try to excuse them by saying this (as some of Churchill's biographers have attempted to do) is too simplistic and naïve. Franco destroyed a democracy rather than have an elected left-wing government in power; Churchill (initially at least) supported Franco for largely the same reason.

1
THE 1920S: THE RAT AND THE KING'S DICTATOR IN PURSUIT OF FOOL'S GOLD

Churchill's hatred of left-wing ideology, to the point of wishful thinking and ignoring facts, was perhaps never better shown than during the Russian civil war. This conflict broke out following the Bolshevik revolution of October/November 1917 and lasted, in terms of British involvement, until 1920. During this time, Churchill and the Liberal led coalition Government supported the White Russian side (a mixture of Tsarist monarchists, liberals, non-Bolshevik socialists and mercenary bandits) as did allied European countries, including France, as well as others from round the world, such as the USA and Japan. Initially, this was done to try to keep Russia in the first World War and defeat Germany. After the armistice of 1918 ended the greater conflict, for people like Churchill, continued military involvement in Russia was about defeating the 'Reds'. As Secretary of State for War, Churchill wanted to "strangle the infant Bolshevism in its cradle".[1] Despite considerable international support, the Whites were defeated by the Bolsheviks. The Whites could never win over the ordinary people of Russia, who feared a return to Tsarist oppression. Churchill was the force behind British intervention in the conflict, in which Britain sent over £100 million worth of military support (more than £4 billion in today's money). British ships, planes, troops and tanks were directly involved in the war,

---

1 Winston Churchill, (said many times including in the House of Commons 1949).

although Churchill did not reveal to Parliament the extent of this and even misled Cabinet colleagues.² He did however tell the House of Commons that he was sending mustard gas to Russia for use against the Bolsheviks, stating that "It is a very right and proper thing to employ poison gas against them."³

Churchill's attitude to the Russian civil war undoubtedly coloured his approach to the Spanish civil war 15 years later. For Churchill, a 'Red' was a 'Red' and he made little distinction between Lenin's Bolshevik revolution and the democratically elected Popular Front government of the Spanish Republic. This clouded his thinking until it was too late. Churchill's lack of appreciation of the differences between various left-wing groups and parties was a failing which created a false understanding of the situation in Spain in the 1930s. In this he was also misled by some of those in Spain, usually British, who were supplying him with information.

Another legacy from the Russian civil war that affected Churchill's thinking later, was his acceptance of the legitimacy of foreign intervention to affect regime change. More than that, Churchill believed that it was acceptable for countries to take military action within another country in support of an idea, or the negation of an idea, as was this case with Bolshevism. This was the same mindset that Mussolini had, and which saw Italian intervention on a massive scale in the Spanish civil war, until the point at which, by 1937, "Italy was effectively at war with the Spanish Republic."⁴ This is over and above Churchill's belief that European countries, and others in a racial hierarchy, were entitled to take over territories by force in order to expropriate their natural resources or exploit their strategic importance.

Spain had taken no part in the First World War although

---

2 Anthony Beevor, *Revolution and Civil War 1917–1921*, p 280.
3 Clive Ponting, *Churchill*, p 237.
4 Paul Preston, *A Concise History of the Spanish Civil War*, p 49.

it faced conflict in its territory of Morocco during the 1920s. The Rif War was fought between Spain and the indigenous tribes of northern Morocco, between 1921 and 1926 (with France aiding the Spanish towards the end of the conflict). The Spanish had been increasingly involved in skirmishes in Morocco for more than a decade, intensified by the treaty of Fes, which carved Morocco up between France and Spain and declared the Rif area a Spanish protectorate in 1912. The fiercely independent Rif tribes resisted the Spanish incursions into their traditional areas, especially when iron ore extraction caused environmental damage and led to the displacement of tribes' people.

The officer class of the Spanish army, bloated and top heavy, displayed corruption and incompetence in Morocco in the early part of the 20th century. Still stung by the loss of almost all of the rest of its empire in 1898, there was a refusal to face the reality of Spain's changed position in the world. Clinging on to the strip of land in North Africa was one of the very few roles left for a military which had once been one of world's great powers. Among the ordinary, conscripted soldiers, there was a great reluctance to fight. Earlier, in 1909, the crushing of a series of protests against conscription in Barcelona resulted in the 'tragic week', when over 100 civilians were killed and over 1700 taken before military courts for acts of rebellion. The anarchists (who were numerically superior in Catalonia among the left) and socialists, objected to working class people, often the sole earner in a family, being conscripted into an army to fight against Moroccans with whom they had no grievance. As the Rif war reignited in the 1920s, the best 'Spanish' troops in Morocco were the *Regulares*, indigenous Moroccans recruited by the Spanish to fight in their army. As problems with conscripts continued, the Spanish recruited more *Regulares* to fight in the Rif war (these troops were to become of central importance in the Spanish civil war). A defeat at Annual in Morocco in 1921, rocked Spain.

Around 3000 Riffian tribesmen had defeated a Spanish force of over 20 000, inflicting more than 13 000 casualties while suffering fewer than 1000 themselves. The disaster was decried as, "the most acute period of Spanish decadence"[5] and highlighted the incompetence of many officers, with an inability to read maps or lead troops. This was the result of men being placed in positions merely because of their family's influence, regardless of their ability. Another criticism made was of the interference of King Alfonso, who had encouraged adventurism which helped lead to the military catastrophe. When told of the defeat and the loss of so many Spanish lives, Alfonso reportedly replied, "chicken meat is cheap" before returning to his game of golf.

One officer who did distinguish himself in Morocco was Francisco Franco. By the end of the Rif war, Franco was promoted to the rank of Brigadier General, at the age of 33, making him the youngest General in Europe. He was known for personal bravery and ruthlessness, especially when dealing with indiscipline. The link between Franco and the troops in Morocco, both legionnaires and *Regulares* (who collectively became known as the Army of Africa), was to prove crucial to his part in the Spanish civil war. Franco's success in the civil war and in his rise to become head of state, owed much to his relationship to the Army of Africa, forged in the Rif war of the 1920s. He was popular with his men because of his meticulousness and his willingness to take the lead when his troops were attacking. Franco had virtually created the Legion, along with Millán-Astray, but when the latter was removed, Franco took exception to being looked over for leadership of the unit and requested a posting on the peninsula (mainland Spain). Franco had become well known through newspaper reports of his successes in Morocco, which an eager public warmed to after the previous military disasters, and he was decorated by the King on his return to Madrid in January

---

5 Socialist deputy, Indalcio Prieto in the Cortes (Spanish parliament).

1923. Franco went back to Morocco only a few months later, as the death in combat of the Legion's new commander led to the King asking Franco to return to Africa to head the Legion.

During the time of the war in Morocco, in September 1923, a military dictatorship, known as the Dictadura, began in Spain. The repressing of a report into the fiasco at Annual, which was going to be critical of the King; and the "lenient" handling of protests against conscription, were the catalyst for the seizing of power by the army general, Miguel Primo de Rivera. Although King Alfonso XIII remained Head of State, Primo de Rivera became a military dictator, not dissimilar to events in Italy happening at the same time; indeed, Alfonso called Primo, "my Mussolini". In Spain, Primo initially ruled through a military directorship and suppressed the press, with heavy censorship. He also opposed demands for Catalan autonomy to the point of banning the Catalan language and flag and cracked down on trade union activity, especially that of the anarchist CNT (*Confederacion Nacional de Trabajos*). The military directorate transformed into a civil directorate in 1925 but in reality, little changed. Primo continued to rule without feeling the need to have elections, even abolishing local government. Primo was opposed to Spanish military action in Morocco and withdrew tens of thousands of Spanish troops in 1923 and again in 1924. Increased action by the Rif tribes led to Primo securing an alliance with France in 1925 which brought an end (successful from a Spanish point of view) to the Rif war.

Attempts at reforms, which were desperately needed in Spain, had mixed success. There was investment in the infrastructure and the economy was partly nationalised, with state monopolies created, but concessions were given to individuals and corporations, and it effectively became state capitalism with a protectionist approach, placing tariffs on imported goods. The investment put into infrastructure came from borrowed money as efforts to introduce a progressive tax system where the rich would pay a little more were rebuffed by the upper classes and subsequently shelved by Primo. Attempts to reform the army to reduce military spending met with opposition from Primo's military colleagues. The internal army reforms which were necessary, such as promotion based on merit and a reduction in the number of officers, were also not progressed by the military directorate. Even more pressing in Spain at this time was the need for agrarian reform. Many of the rural workers lived a precarious life, with intermittent, low paid work. By contrast, some landowners had little interest in the efficient use of their land and would rather keep prize bills in comfort than produce food. By the end of the 1920s, "half of Spain went to bed hungry." Meanwhile in Britain, Churchill lost his Dundee seat in the election of 1922 to a socialist, prohibitionist candidate (the first and only prohibitionist MP ever elected in Britain), and again lost, standing as a Liberal for the final time, in Leicester in 1923. Churchill then stood as an independent "anti-socialist" candidate and made it a hat-trick of election losses in two years when he failed to win the Westminster Abbey by-election in 1924. This meant that Churchill was not in the House of Commons during the administration of the historic first Labour Government under Ramsey MacDonald. Until 1922, Churchill had been a Liberal MP for 16 years, being an important part of the great, reforming Liberal Government which helped to set the foundations of a welfare state prior to the first World War. Churchill was clear that his prime motivation was to stave off the growth of the Labour Party and that social reform by the Liberals meant stopping socialism by the Labour Party by appeasing the masses.

    During his period outside of the Commons in the 1920s, Churchill was moving closer and closer to going back to the Conservatives, the party he had left for the Liberals twenty years before. At the general election of October 1924, which ended the minority Labour Government's term, Churchill was elected as an independent "Constitutionalist" but crucially had the backing of the Conservatives. By the following year, Churchill had formally re-joined the Conservatives, whom he had left for the Liberals in 1904. As he said himself, conscious of the distrust that many on all sides now regarded him with, "Anyone can rat, but it takes a certain ingenuity to re-rat."[6]

When the Conservatives returned to government following the October 1924 election, Churchill was rewarded by Prime Minister Stanley Baldwin by being given the post of Chancellor of the Exchequer. Churchill as Chancellor was not a success and his time in office provoked much criticism. One of the most damning allegations was that his mandating of cuts in defence spending and subsequent disarmament helped substantially to bring about the crisis of the 1930s, during which, Churchill was demanding that Britain re-armed. Far from shouldering some of the blame for this a decade later, Churchill displayed breath-taking hypocrisy. As Chancellor in the 1920s, Churchill had argued, to Prime Minister Baldwin, that rearmament could bring about not only war but another Labour Government (a far worse outcome in Churchill's eyes). When Baldwin used a similar argument as to why he did not rearm before 1935, Churchill later accused him of putting party before country.[7] As Chancellor, Churchill argued against the Admiralty's expansionist plans for the Far East, not wishing to antagonise the Japanese and has been blamed by some more specifically for not bolstering Singapore's defences at that time, helping to lead to the disaster suffered there by the British during the second World War.

More than the impact on defence spending and the consequences that this may have had, Churchill's Chancellorship

---

6 Andrew Roberts, *Churchill*, p 309.
7 Andrew Roberts, *Churchill*, p 310.

is also remembered for his disastrous decision to join the Gold Standard in 1925. The effects on the economy helped create the conditions for the General Strike in 1926, which was directly caused by Churchill's budget of that year, which ended a coal subsidy. The mine owners reacted by wanting to simultaneously increase the hours and decrease the wages of coal miners in Britain. The miners were locked-out but supported by the TUC resulting in a General Strike less than a week after the budget, which lasted for nine days. The result was the largest, concentrated effort of the organised working class in Britain, but ultimate defeat for both the strike and the miners. During this time, Churchill revelled in his role as class-warrior and was responsible for producing the Government's propaganda newspaper, The British Gazette, since the strike had prevented most newspaper production. Churchill entered into this with customary gusto. Calling strikers, "the enemy" Churchill likened the industrial strife to a war, and for Churchill it was. Moderate Labour politicians like George Lansbury were virtually indistinguishable to Churchill from Bolsheviks from Moscow and Churchill even wanted to commandeer the BBC (he need hardly have bothered since the BBC took the Government's side). Churchill's reputation as an enemy of the working class was secured.

The worsening economic situation in the world towards the end of the 1920s affected Britain and Spain both financially and politically. In 1928, before the crash which plunged the rest of the world into economic chaos, the Spanish peseta collapsed. Spain's right wing finance Minister, Jose Calvo Sotelo, who had been appointed by Primo, pegged the Spanish currency to the Gold Standard, as Chancellor Churchill had done with Sterling, with even more disastrous consequences. As many of the Spanish elite turned lukewarm towards Primo's regime, elsewhere in the country the desire for genuine political change was moving towards a tipping point. The left-wing groupings

The 1920s

were joined by liberal, middle class, anti-clerical republicans and even conservative politicians and some army officers in a growing movement which demanded both an end to the reign of Alfonso and the establishment of a proper democracy. There could be no return to the corrupt "Tweedledum Tweedledee" of the *Turno Pacifico*, which preceded the Dictadura, where the two main parties took it in turn to rule with no impetus for modernisation or for much needed reform. There had to be a serious attempt to make Spain democratic in order to avoid a catastrophe for an increasingly alienated monarchy. Unfortunately, Alfonso chose to accept Primo's resignation in January 1930 and replace him with another General, Berenguer. For those seeking reform, this was the last straw.

In Britain, Churchill's less than successful tenure as Chancellor came to an end with the dissolution of the Baldwin Government prior to the general election in May 1929. Before this, Churchill had shown his preference for fascism over communism during his visit to Mussolini's Italy, where he was fulsome in his praise for the Italian dictator. Somewhat staggeringly, the British Chancellor of the Exchequer heaped praise on Mussolini's economic policies, believing that Mussolini "has the courage to impose the financial remedies required to secure and stabilize the national recovery."[8]

Bad enough that the person in charge of the British economy should be an admirer of the fascist dictator but worse was to come when Churchill met Mussolini in Rome in early 1927 and was unstinting in his praise for the dictator and his movement, saying that fascism had:

"...rendered service to the whole world. If I had been an Italian, I am sure I would have been wholeheartedly with you

---

8 Robert Rhodes James, *Winston S. Churchill: His Complete Speeches IV*, p 3821.

from start to finish in your triumphant struggle."[9]

Once again and certainly not for the last time, Churchill's hatred of the Left blinded him to the threat posed by fascism. Even the most sycophantic of Churchill's biographers struggle to excuse his comments on Mussolini. Some point out that the triumphant struggle that Churchill spoke of was against communism, in his opinion. That it was also against democracy and in pursuit of fascism was a price Churchill clearly believed was worth paying. More shallow renderings of history conflate Churchill's fondness for Mussolini with the policy in the 1930s, supported by Churchill, of trying to prevent fascist Italy from allying with Nazi Germany. This policy, part of the overall appeasement approach to Europe in the 1930s, was not relevant in the 1920s when Churchill was praising Mussolini.

In the "Flapper Election" of May 1929 (the first in which women aged 21-29 had the vote), the Labour Party emerged with the highest number of seats for the first time ever, but short of an overall majority. Although Churchill retained his seat, the Conservatives were out of power and a minority Labour Government took over, unfortunately only months before the Wall Street crash would plunge the world into economic chaos. Churchill was on an extended (three month) North American holiday and lecture tour when the crash happened and it was a personal blow to him as he had speculated in stocks and shares, including in the USA when on his travels. By a quirk of fate and the knack that he seemed to have for being in the thick of the action, Churchill was actually on Wall Street when the crash happened and was in a hotel as a stockbroker jumped to his death on the street outside. Churchill lost the money he had made on his lecture tour and more that he had earned from writing, including advances. He returned home, still a member of the

---

9 Martin Gilbert, *Winston S. Churchill: The Coming of War 1922-1939*, p 226.

Shadow Cabinet but feeling poorer and effectively powerless. He did have a new cause on a familiar theme. When he was absent, the Shadow Cabinet under Baldwin had agreed to support the Labour Government's decision to grant dominion status to India. Opposing this was to become his chief political concern over the next few years, combining as it did his love of Empire and hatred of the Left, as it had been proposed by MacDonald.

As the Twenties drew to a close, both Britain and Spain were on the brink of massive political changes which were to help shape the whole of the 1930s in both countries. For Churchill and Franco however, they were little more than observers to the momentous events about to unfold.

2
CHANGING OF THE GUARD: BRITAIN AND SPAIN 1930-1931

The Pact of San Sebastian brought together a very disparate group of individuals and organisations with a common cause: to end the rule of the Spanish monarchy and establish a Spanish republic. Although ranging from conservatives to socialists, those involved had a singularity of belief that Spain could only progress if it first got rid of Alfonso XIII. The republicans gathered in the northern Spanish city of San Sebastian in August 1930 to form a revolutionary committee, effectively a republican government in waiting. An aborted attempt to overturn the regime by a group of republican army officers in December of that year merely resulted in creating two republican martyrs, Captains, Fermin Galán and Ángel Garcia Hernández, when the unfortunate pair of Captains, who did not realise the uprising had been postponed, were executed for their actions. The writing was on the wall for Alfonso though and it seemed clear to virtually everyone except the King and his closest aristocratic allies, that the Spanish monarchy was doomed.

Francisco Franco's brother, Ramón, did not share his military sibling's love of monarchy and was part of the revolutionary plot of December 1930. Ramón had married in 1924 without seeking the King's permission, contrary to etiquette and highlighting the difference between the siblings. Ramón had become a Spanish national hero in 1926 when he flew across the Atlantic from Spain to Argentina, even eclipsing the fame of his military hero brother, Francisco, in the public eye for a while. However, Ramón had very different political views to his traditionalist brother. Ramón was a syndicalist and attracted to the anarchist end of the Spanish political spectrum. Immediately following the execution of the two army Captains for their part in the failed coup, Ramón flew over Madrid, dropping leaflets proclaiming a republican revolution. He was also apparently prepared to bomb the royal palace but was put off by the presence of civilians. He escaped to Portugal where he remained until the Spanish Republic was proclaimed a few months later.

In Britain, the economic crisis deepened in 1930, as the world plunged into the Great Depression that was to last for several years, and the Labour Government struggled to cope with its effects. The list of demands from its supporters and the Party was extensive, as usually follows the election of a left-wing government. The budget in 1930 and other pieces of legislation, provided for increased spending in many areas, including education. However, the Cabinet's approach was one of economic orthodoxy, which was increasingly unable to cope with an unprecedented financial crash. The Government was put under extreme pressure from international finance to 'balance the books' and curtail the amount spent on unemployment benefits, which was multiplying as more were put out of work. The only way the government could have done this would have been to lower the amount of benefit payable.

In Spain, political strikes and university protests were openly calling for the abolition of the monarchy and for the establishment of a democratic republic. Panicking at the inability of his appointee to stem the growing republican tide, Alfonso sacked Berenguer and replaced him with Admiral Aznar, in February 1931. Giving a sop to the movement for democracy, in a vain attempt to stop the republican juggernaut, municipal elections were announced for April 1931. This was to be the start of a very gradual move to a representative government, but the people had other ideas about the pace of change required. The elections were meant to be producing local councils as the first tentative step, but the multi-party system which was permitted saw many parties standing as openly republican, even though in theory the elections could have no bearing on the national picture. When the voters spoke, Alfonso's days were numbered.

On the evening of 12th April, as the results came in, it was clear that the pro republican parties had won handsomely in what had effectively become a referendum on the future of the monarchy. As virtually all the main municipalities were won by parties aligned to the revolutionary committee, crowds took to the streets to proclaim a republic. Alcalá-Zamora, the conservative politician who headed the revolutionary committee was being called upon to take over as the head of a new government, despite the municipal elections having nothing directly to do with the Cortes, (the Spanish Parliament) and still less concerned with appointing a head of state. The army was instructed to abide by the will of the people, as tensions rose, and civil war seemed a possibility. The head of the Civil Guard, (a paramilitary police force so often used to suppress industrial and peasant unrest), General Sanjurjo, was asked if the King could count on his support. However, Sanjurjo was still angered by being passed over when Berenguer had been chosen by the King to replace Primo. Alfonso was told he could not count on the support of the Civil Guard to oppose the will of the people: Sanjurjo had his revenge. The Aznar Government resigned en masse. The King fled Spain and the second Spanish Republic was declared on the 14th of April 1931.

Churchill was devastated by the departure of the Spanish King. He commiserated with Alfonso, who seemed bewildered by the lack of support from his subjects shown in the municipal elections. Churchill said that Alfonso likened the shock of learning that he was not supported by the Spanish people "to going to call upon an old friend and found that he was dead." Churchill was annoyed that municipal elections had become a plebiscite on the monarchy and also believed that the King had been premature in stepping down because the election results, when known in full, would have shown a majority favoured Alfonso and the retention of monarchy.

"The actual crisis came suddenly, unexpectedly, upon a false issue, as a result of mere municipal elections, into which the fundamental question ought never to have entered. Even so, there was a large monarchical majority; but no one waited for the final result. The crisis came attended by every circumstance of violence and affront."[1]

Churchill was incorrect in every regard. The republican forces achieved double the number of seats that the monarchist parties did, despite the corruption that persisted in areas in the countryside ruled over by landowners who bribed, intimidated and bullied landless peasants into supporting their candidates. The Republicans won control of virtually every major city and the declaration of the Republic was a spontaneous and joyous occasion, far removed from the violence and affront of Churchill's imagination.

Franco greeted the coming of the new Republic with undisguised disdain, but he was not about to do anything that would jeopardise his own career. By this time, Franco was the head of the officer training Academy at Zaragoza, having overseen its construction and the intake of the first batch of new recruits in 1928. During the abortive uprising of December 1930, as his brother sought to bring down the monarchy, Franco armed his recruits and put them on alert to counter any popular challenge to the King and his regime. Franco was not going to commit any self-harm to his career however and grudgingly permitted the

---
1 Winston Churchill, *Great Contemporaries*, p 158-159.

flying of the new Spanish tricolour, once he had received written orders that he must do so. The provisional government in Spain was hardly the stuff of the Bolshevik nightmares of Churchill's imagination. It was headed by a Conservative, Niceto Alcalá-Zamora and largely made-up of politicians who would have been more at home in the Liberal Party if they were in Britain, rather than anywhere else. Indeed, the provisional government was a balance of the main republican groups and had centre-right, centre and centre left as well as some members of the PSOE, the Spanish Socialist Workers Party, approximately equivalent to the British Labour Party but with a more radical left-wing.

As debate over the new Spanish constitution continued throughout the year, the Spanish Right and traditionalists were horrified at what seemed like a rapid pace of change. Two elements in the proposed constitution particularly alarmed the less radical members of the government, including Alcalá-Zamora and Miguel Maura. These were the stripping from the Catholic Church of its traditional privileges within Spain and the provision for expropriation of land in certain circumstances. For these two centre-right politicians, it was the "attacks" on the church that they deemed unacceptable to their Catholic electorate. The separation of Church and State was carried out with a certain zeal by anti-clerical politicians such as Manuel Azaña. In October 1931, Alcalá-Zamora and Maura left the government, with the Liberal, Azaña becoming Prime Minister. Alcalá-Zamora however became President of the second Spanish Republic on 10th December, following the adoption of the new constitution, and remained in post until April 1936.

Both Britain and Spain held general elections in 1931 and each heralded a new era. In Spain, following nearly a decade of dictatorship and the memory of the sham of democracy which existed prior to that, the June 1931 election was seen as the first proper general election the country had ever had. Women would be given the right to vote under the new constitution, which was to be decided by the new Cortes, and therefore could not vote in the 1931 election, although they could stand as candidates. The new electoral system favoured coalitions of parties as they were effectively given extra seats if they could gain a majority in an area. This system was designed to try to ensure cooperation, but the increasing polarisation of Spanish society in the 1930s meant that at this and each subsequent election, opposing camps vied to gain a small majority of the votes which would translate into a larger majority of seats.

The British general election of the same year did not have quite as dramatic a backdrop but still marked a fundamental shift in the political landscape. Against the worsening economic crisis, the minority Labour Government of Ramsey MacDonald was split on cuts to public expenditure, particularly the 'need' to cut unemployment benefit. At what seemed an impasse, MacDonald resigned as Prime Minister on 24th August but was then reappointed by the King in order to form a new government to tackle to economic collapse. This government was intended to be able to draw upon the best talents in parliament, regardless of party, as the country was deemed to be facing a national emergency. The bulk of the Labour Party refused to join the new National Government and MacDonald, Labour's first and at that point only, Prime Minster, was expelled from the party. The Conservatives under Baldwin supported and joined the National Government, but without a place in that Government for Churchill. Winston had previously resigned from the Shadow Cabinet after clashing publicly with Baldwin over the Conservative leader's support for Labour's policy of granting Dominion status to India. This issue was, more than any other, the main cause of Churchill's wilderness years. Churchill's stubborn refusal to allow India any form of self-governance put him at odds with most, including a majority of fellow Conservatives. Churchill was therefore not invited to be part of the National Government, though he had not yet given up hope of being given a portfolio at some stage.

The National Government felt that it needed the legitimacy of a mandate and called a general election in October 1931. This caused Lloyd George to remove part of the Liberal Party from the National Government to stand as Independent Liberals, with others who remained loyal to the National Government standing as National Liberals and as Liberals as the party was now split three ways. The Conservatives went into the election more united than they had been for some time. Although India and protectionism were still bones of contention, this was a chance to return to power and it galvanised the Party. Churchill swallowed his misgivings about a National Government which put the Conservatives in bed with MacDonald, in return for the possibility of a place in the Cabinet. He supported the party policy at the election.

The new electoral freedom in Spain saw a plethora of parties and alliances, many of them hastily formed, as the various strands and interest groupings in Spanish society vied for electoral support. Again, contrary to Churchill's belief, even though he wrote with the benefit of hindsight, there was very little support for monarchist politicians in the elections. Monarchist parties won just 10 of the 470 seats contested in the summer of 1931. The largest grouping was the Marxist left and anarchists who won 125 seats, with the PSOE gaining 115 of these; the republican parties of the left gained 124 seats; The Nationalist Left won 44 seats. Republican parties of the centre and right won 129 seats, however the largest party within this, Alejandro Lerroux's Radical Republican Party, who emerged with 90 representatives in the Cortes, supported the centre-left coalition government. Nationalist and regionalist parties of the centre and right took 20 seats; while a further 20 were won by right wing parties. The parties and individuals who had formed the Pact of San Sebastien and subsequently the provisional government, had been legitimised by the electorate. They forged ahead with drafting the new constitution and initiating reforms. The results of the UK general election, held in October were also historic. The landslide for the National Government was colossal. The biggest winners were the Conservatives who, unlike their rivals, were united. They emerged with 470 of the 554 seats won by the National Government, who gained two-thirds of the popular vote. MacDonald's National Labour took just 13 seats. Both the National Government supporting groups of Liberals took more than 30 seats each. The opposition Labour Party won only 52 seats; Lloyd George's Independent Liberals took 4 seats and there were only another 5 MPs in Parliament not on the National Government ticket. Despite the weight of Conservatives within the National Government, Ramsey MacDonald remained as Prime Minister.

Churchill was returned in his Epping constituency with an increased majority. Despite his pre-election hopes, Churchill was never likely to gain a place in MacDonald's cabinet as Winston found it difficult to disguise his dislike for the Scottish Premier. There was a class element to this but that is too simplistic to explain Churchill's antagonism. Roy Jenkins puts Churchill's attitude down to MacDonald's views on India as Ramsey was in favour of moving towards self-government but also to Churchill's disdain for the "sham" of the National Government, fuelled by his exclusion from it. There was more to it than even this, although that undoubtedly added to Churchill's attitude. The India issue was never far from the front of Churchill's mind as protection of the Empire was one of his two overriding political preoccupations. Churchill's contempt for Gandhi is well known, calling him, "A seditious Middle Temple lawyer now posing as a fakir"[2] in 1931 as part of his explanation for resignation from the Shadow Cabinet. Being left out by Macdonald and the others only added fuel to the fire of Churchill's hatred of MacDonald, but it did not ignite it. In January 1931, months before the coalition government was formed, Churchill attacked MacDonald in the House of Commons in a speech where he compared the Labour Prime Minister to a freak in Barnum's circus, specifically, the boneless wonder. It is much more likely that, along with India, it was MacDonald's opposition to the First World War was the main cause of Churchill's vitriol. By contrast, when Attlee became Labour leader, Churchill remarked that he had a fine war record.

In Alcalá-Zamora's cabinet in the provisional government in Spain, established in April and legitimised by the June elections, Manuel Azaña was made Minister of War. Azaña was head of the Republican Action party, which he had founded in 1926 along with José Giral. A writer and lawyer, Azaña was regarded as an intellectual and was vehemently anti-clerical. In charge of Spain's armed forces, Azaña had to reduce the vast amount of the country's wealth that was spent on the top-heavy army. During the worldwide depression and with so many competing priorities for investment in the new republic, curtailing the cost the army was a top priority. With the highest officer to men ration of any army, it seemed obvious to any independent observer that the officer corps had to be reduced. One of Azaña's actions in pursuit of this in the summer of 1931 was to have a profound effect on Franco and start a lifelong hatred of Azaña by the General. The Minister of War announced that the military academy at Zaragoza which trained officers was to close, partly because of the cost but also because it was a breeding ground for traditionalist politics and many in it had monarchist beliefs. Franco was shocked. As the

---

2 Robert Rhodes James, *Winston S. Churchill: His Complete Speeches V,* p 4985.

head of the academy, Franco had prided himself on the discipline he had instilled into the young officers and was convinced that he was producing the next generation of defenders of the Patria. The decision was one which Franco never forgave Azaña for.

In his farewell speech to the recruits at the Academy in July, Franco's bitterness was clear. He made not very well disguised attacks on Azaña and those that the politician had appointed to high positions within the military. There were tears in his eyes when he took the acclaim of the cadets at the end. Azaña was less impressed with the speech when he read a copy of it, the Minister of War noting that the speech would have been, "a case for instant dismissal, if it were not the case that today he ceased to hold that command."[3] Azaña contented himself with placing an official reprimand on Franco's record. When Alcalá-Zamora resigned as Prime Minster in the Autumn, it was Azaña who took over, while retaining his Minister of War portfolio. Franco was now without a proper role and faced with a Prime Minister and Minister of War whom he despised on a personal and political level.

As 1931 drew to a close, both Spain and Britain had newly formed, coalition governments. Each was trying to find a way out of the consequences of the world economic collapse and both had a further weight of expectations. In Britain, the National Government had to plot their recovery against the backdrop of increasing instability in Europe, especially political division in Germany and the belligerent military expansionism of Italy. Britain had not come to terms with its role in the post First World War era of extremism and the rise of Pacific powers in the USA and Japan. The desire for peace was uppermost in most British minds but the projection of power to preserve that peace was costly. Churchill was sulking, out of government and

---

3 Manuel Azaña, *Obras completes de Manuel Azaña*, Volume IV, 16, 22 July 1931, pp. 33, 39.

seemingly out of touch, with his views on India at odds with most of his parliamentary contemporaries. Churchill also alienated some with his praise of Mussolini and indifference – at best - to Japanese Imperial expansionism. In Spain, with Alcalá-Zamora now installed as President and Azaña's Government endorsed by the new constitution, the real battles for the future of the country were just beginning. Armed with a long list of reforms demanded by an eager population, the pressure on Azaña and his colleagues was great. The new Spain seemed to be leaving traditionalists like Franco behind and his meteoric rise in the army had been halted abruptly. The constitution of the Republic, adopted in December 1931, did not mention the army and in the new Spain there was to be no special place for the armed forces who had created and crushed regimes in the country on several occasions over the previous century. Azaña said that "No one now speaks of the army, nor does the army speak for itself." Franco and others were to prove that the pronouncement on the death of the army as a force in Spanish politics was premature.

3
LOOKING LEFT WHEN THE DANGER WAS FROM THE RIGHT: CHURCHILL IN THE WILDERNESS AND THE SECOND REPUBLIC AT 'PEACE'

Churchill went to America again in December 1931 and was in New York for another 'crash'. This time the effects on him were more than just financial as he almost lost his life when he was knocked over. Churchill had been crossing Fifth Avenue and was halfway over the road when he forgot about the direction of traffic in America. He recuperated in Barbados after being released from hospital in New York. A scar on his forehead would be a permanent reminder of Churchill looking left when the danger was from the right.

Although later remembered as being vehemently opposed to dictators and their regimes, Churchill did not treat all of that ilk the same. In 1933, Churchill called Mussolini, "The greatest lawgiver among men."[1] Churchill was also full of praise for Japan in 1931, despite it having recently invaded Manchuria. As Churchill's biographer, Andrew Roberts states, "As with Mussolini, he allowed his anti-Communism to blur his

---

1 Martin Gilbert, *Winston S. Churchill: The Coming of War 1922-1939*, p 457.

judgement."[2] A very mild rebuke considering this is Churchill praising despotic, fascist regimes and their leaders in the 1930s and one that could only be contemplated by pardoning Churchill retrospectively because of wartime leadership. This is a common error among most of those who write about Churchill. The leadership he gave in World War II is allowed to excuse every other action he takes almost regardless of how ill-judged it was. Leaving aside an assessment of Churchill's premiership, any attempt to give retrospective absolution means that his actions and words before 1940 are not given proper scrutiny. The mythologising of Churchill as a lone voice of anti-appeasement in the 1930s is inaccurate on both counts. Churchill was far from the only person speaking up against the Nazi and fascist threats facing European democracies and elsewhere around the world. More than this however, Churchill was far from consistent in opposing fascism nor in always being anti-appeasement. In his biography of Churchill, Jenkins, states that Churchill, "always saw the threat to Britain's security as essentially a German threat. He was therefore equivocal on what he regarded as peripheral challenges to the world order, from the Japanese invasion of Manchuria in 1931 through Mussolini's Abyssinian adventure in 1935 to the civil war in Spain in 1936-9".[3] This again shows that Churchill was not an anti-appeaser, or even an antifascist. Churchill believed in the right of strong countries to dominate weaker ones, after all, this was the basis of empire.

Japan's invasion and occupation of Manchuria and the establishment of the puppet state of Manchukuo were condemned by the League of Nations in the otherwise timid Lytton report. However, Japan took no notice and walked out, firstly of the League of Nations meeting discussing the report and subsequently the League itself. The episode showed the

---

2 Andrew Roberts, *Churchill*, p 366.
3 Roy Jenkins, *Churchill*, p 464.

weakness of the League of Nations. It also highlighted Churchill's willingness to overlook the aggression of countries provided their governments were not left wing. In the aftermath of Japan's militarism against China, Churchill urged people in Britain to think more kindly of Japan, despite its aggression, because, "On the one side they see the dark menace of Soviet Russia. On the other, the chaos of China, four or five provinces of which are now being tortured under Communist rule."[4] As with Spain some years later, Churchill was caught out looking left when the danger was from the right.

The realities of government and the weight of expectation were beginning to be felt greatly by Azaña and his coalition of supporters in 1932. Poor economic conditions around the world and bad harvests in Spain added to their woes. The Left, especially those outside of the government including the anarchists, were demanding rapid and radical change, firstly to land ownership. Meanwhile, the Right-wing press and traditional establishment reacted to every reform as if the government were transforming Spain into a Bolshevist state, which they most certainly were not. Landowners refused to implement new laws and the Civil Guard in the countryside invariably took their side against the peasants. Facing these pressures from both sides, Azaña's government were given an unexpected boost to their support by a sharp reminder to everyone of what the alternative to the Republic might be.

General Sanjurjo, whose lack of commitment to supporting the King with the Civil Guard had helped to hasten the end for Alfonso, had not warmed to the regime which replaced the Monarchy. In the summer of 1931, along with a number of other officers, Sanjurjo began plotting a coup against the Republican Government. This became serious in 1932 after incidents in which Civil Guards, the force that Sanjurjo was

---

4 Robert Rhodes James, *Winston S. Churchill: His Complete Speeches V,* p 5220.

head of, killed unarmed protestors or strikers (some Civil Guard officers had also been killed in one incident where the crowd took revenge). Azaña had reacted by getting rid of Sanjurjo as the Commander of the Civil Guard and effectively demoting him to a lesser position. This brought some sympathy for Sanjurjo among other army officers and the plotting against Azaña intensified.

The conspiracy in the summer of 1932 was known to Azaña, who ensured that loyal commanders and army units were placed at strategic points to counteract the uprising. The result was that in August 1932, the attempted coup was a complete failure. In Madrid it started early in the morning and was over by 8am, with little loss of life and most rebels captured. Elsewhere, with the exception of Seville, the coup was even less eventual, with almost nothing happening. It was where Sanjurjo was to lead the plotters, in Seville, that the whole conspiracy had its only – very short lived – success. For under 24 hours he took control of the southern city with a small group of armed men but was forced to flee as forces loyal to the government approached. Seville was won and lost by the plotters without a shot being fired. Sanjurjo was arrested on his way to the Portuguese border. He was later sentenced to death, but this was commuted.

The relief felt by ordinary people that the coup had been thwarted led to an upsurge in support for the ideal of a republic and for the programme of the government. On the back of this, Azaña's Government were able to make progress on some reforms which had become bogged down in the Cortes and also confiscated some land to be redistributed, despite complaints that a number of the landowners targeted for this had not had anything to do with the plot. Franco had wisely not taken part in the doomed Sanjurjada (as the plot became mockingly known as), indeed he had not even signed a petition in favour of Sanjurjo following the demotion from Head of the Civil Guard. Sanjurjo had met with Franco prior to the doomed uprising and attempted to recruit him to the plot. Franco refused to have anything to do with it and had a thinly disguised criticism of Sanjurjo's part in Alfonso's downfall, saying that since the army had defected from the monarchy's cause it could hardly be expected to change sides. Before the coup however, Sanjurjo and others believed that Franco would rise with them and it seems that Franco was at least ambiguous about his intentions when he met Sanjurjo only a month before the coup. Sanjurjo later remarked from prison that Franco only looked after himself.[5] Having correctly judged that the plot was doomed, Franco was certainly not going to have his name attached to it retrospectively. Franco refused to appear as Sanjurjo's defender when requested and rather callously remarked that to him that since Sanjurjo had rebelled and failed, he had, "earned the right to die."[6]

After a gap when the Republic was not quite sure what to do with him, following his loss of the position as Head of the Military Academy when it was closed, Franco was appointed to La Coruna as Commander of the Galician infantry stationed there in February 1932, several months before the Sanjurjada. Close to his family home, Franco was able visit his mother every weekend. Azaña had believed that Franco had been rehabilitated and was now loyal to the Republic. In fact, Franco harboured an intense dislike of the new regime and a loathing of Azaña in particular. A review of promotions hung over Franco's head for two years and although in the end he did not suffer any actual demotion, the worry and the minor humiliation he endured only added to his feelings towards Azaña.

For Churchill also, this period was a low point. Although a Conservative MP in a House of Commons where his party was

---

5 Eugenio Vegas Latapie, *La frustración en la Victoria: memorias politicas*, p 184.
6 Rogelio Baon, *La cara humana de un caudillo*, p 110.

by far the largest, he was as far from office as he had ever been. The continuation of the National Government left very little hope that Churchill would gain a position in government, far less in the Cabinet. MacDonald as Prime Minister made that virtually certain, however Churchill's views on India had also distanced himself from many of his own Conservative Party colleagues. Churchill remained highly critical of the National Government and not just because he was not in it. Writing retrospectively, he stated that, "The British Government… was in appearance one of the strongest and in fact one of the weakest in British records."[7]

Churchill first warned of the threat of war and the need to prevent British defence spending cuts in a speech in the House of Commons in May 1932. It was clear to Churchill then that Germany was the threat that the country should guard against. As Hitler took power in 1933, this began to become Churchill's new obsession: that Germany was a threat and that Britain had to re-arm to be prepared for the war to come. With the benefit of hindsight, this seems prophetic, and it is certainly true that there was no eager audience to listen to Churchill on this in the early 1930s. Churchill believed that the 1920s consensus that had developed, once the fever of Versailles had subsided, that Germany should be raised up to be a peaceful and prosperous neighbour, was no longer valid. Achieving peace by each country having an approximate equivalence of arms, which could be said to be a fair summing up of the British Government position in the early 1930s, was now bankrupt. Churchill had not agreed with the policy but argued that now that German democracy had been swept away to be replaced by the "most grim dictatorship"[8] the argument was moribund. MacDonald's plan to bring about European disarmament was left in tatters in October 1933, when Hitler refused to accept the terms and withdrew not only from

---
7 Winston Churchill, *The Gathering Storm*, p 60.
8 Winston Churchill, *The Gathering Storm*, p 69.

the disarmament conference but from the League of Nations.

Churchill's obsession with India, battling against any form of home rule far less full independence, continued to take up much of his political time and he formed a group of likeminded MPs called, "The India Defence League", though it was defending Britain's imperial interests in India rather than the country itself. It could be argued that this overshadowed and harmed Churchill's warnings of the threat of Germany and that he might have found a more receptive audience if he had not been denying democracy in India. This however is an argument that can only be made in hindsight and one that there is little evidence for in any case. There were very few others in Britain who were calling for Britain to re-arm in 1933 and the desire to avoid war, at virtually any cost, was prevalent.

In Spain, 1933 ended with a twist in the growth of the country as a democratic Republic that not many could have foreseen: the Left lost control. The year had started badly for Azaña, as continued sporadic insurrection by anarchists had led to an incident at Casas Viejas, near Cadiz, which left 22 peasants and 3 from the security forces dead. The Left was split between wanting to restore law and order and anger at the loss of civilian life at the hands of Civil and Assault Guards representing Azaña's government. There was faux outrage from the Right about the brutality, after having demanded a crackdown. Azaña and his government suffered greatly as a result and deteriorated further until President Alcalá-Zamora called for fresh elections to be held in November. The Left entered the contest in disarray and fragmented. These were the first national elections held under the new constitution meaning that women could vote. The Right were more unified than ever, and a new force emerged: the *Confederación Española de Derechas Autónomas* (CEDA) which was established as a Catholic defence movement aiming to reverse the anti-clerical clauses of the constitution. Led by

Jose Maria Gil-Robles, the party became the rallying point for the Right. Gil-Robles was an admirer of Hitler and the Nazis and visited Germany to study their methods. The key to winning any election in the second republic era was the formation of an electoral coalition. The electoral system had been modified earlier that year and meant in any area even a simple plurality would handsomely reward the coalition gaining it and for a coalition getting even a small majority in an area, they would get 80% of the seats. The results showed the Left the folly of being disunited.

The PSOE lost almost half its seats, ending with 59. Lerroux's centre leaning Radical Republican Party were the only one who had supported the governing coalition who were big winners as they had switched support away from Azaña's grouping and won 104 seats, almost double that of the PSOE on only half of the number of votes. It was CEDA who emerged as the single biggest party with 115 seats. President Alcalá-Zamora appointed Lerroux to lead a government, consisting entirely of Radical Party colleagues, however, they had to rely on CEDA votes in the Cortes to pass anything. This meant that even out of government, Gil Robles was exerting an influence, which greatly worried the Left. The strongest socialist party in Europe had just been abolished in Germany by Hitler, and Gil Robles did little to hide his admiration for both the substance and tactics of the Nazis. He believed that democracy was only a means to an end and participation in elections was using the system in order to get the power to destroy it. This was the "accidentalist" school of thought and contrasted with the "catastrophist" beliefs of others on the far right who wanted a coup to seize power. In early 1934 however, the accidentalists seemed to have the reins among the Right. The influence of Gil Robles meant the government started to reverse the reforms of the previous two years and gave immunity to those who had taken part in the Sanjurjada.

Looking Left When the Danger was from the Right

President Alcalá-Zamora was very reluctant to give this latter measure consent and during the stand-off, in April 1934, Lerroux offered his resignation, which Alcalá-Zamora accepted, replacing him with his Radical Party colleague, Ricardo Samper. Alcalá-Zamora gave his consent to the amnesty and for now CEDA were content to back the government without being represented in it. This uneasy settlement could not last. The semi-autonomous Catalan government were resisting attempts by Samper's government to reverse land reform in their area. Tensions simmered throughout the summer of 1934. The repeal of the Law of municipal boundaries meant that landowners were once again free to bring in cheap labour, from Portugal and elsewhere, to collect the harvest. Many peasants were left literally starving and only given work if they ripped up their union membership card. Others begging for food were told to 'eat the Republic'. Events came to a head in October. Frustrated by the lack of progress (as they saw it) of the Government's programme and faced with Catalan resistance and a number of industrial disputes by both the anarchist CNT and the socialist UGT, CEDA declared they were withdrawing support from the Government unless they were represented in the cabinet. Samper resigned and Alcalá-Zamora had to bring back Lerroux as Prime Minister. Lerroux announced his new cabinet, with three CEDA members in it. This predictably caused an armed uprising from the Left; in fact, this was exactly what Gil Robles and the interior minister, Salazar Alonso wanted. The latter had been largely responsible for causing the hunger in the countryside and both he and Gil Robles knew that the Left, despite their rhetoric, were not prepared for an armed struggle. The result was that the uprising was an uprising damp squib in most places and easily crushed elsewhere, with one exception. In the Asturias there were two factors which combined to mean that, for a few days at least, the uprising did take hold. One was that the miners there had access to explosives and some small arms pilfered from factories. The second was that there was cooperation among socialists, anarchists and others which ensured that they were able to coordinate their plans. This northerly area could not hold out alone however and the Asturias uprising was brutally put down. A state of martial law was declared in the area and General Franco was effectively put in charge of regaining control. This gave Franco an intoxicating taste of being the military-political leader of a region and almost total control and carte blanche to do as he pleased. Franco brought in the Army of Africa and used heavy artillery to bring the miners to submission. The reprisals were akin to the brutality used against Moroccan tribes, with soldiers raping women, torturing prisoners and carrying out summary executions. In the aftermath, 30 000 were imprisoned and the statute of autonomy of Catalonia was repealed as they had, separately, declared independence, but without the support of the anarchists and crucially not arming the workers to defend their new state.

As Spain entered 1935, Franco was the undoubted hero of the Right and secure in the knowledge that he was supported at the very height of government. Spain moved rightward, with Lerroux unable to stop increased CEDA representation in his cabinet. Shamefully, the Radical Party leader contended himself with continued corruption which enriched himself, his friends and political cronies. Meanwhile Churchill was privately content with his enforced inaction, continually warning against German military expansion and calling for Britain to arm itself while working on building projects at his Chartwell home. As long as MacDonald remained Prime Minister, Churchill knew he would not be in government, but the former Labour leader's days as Prime Minister were numbered.

4
THE CALM BEFORE THE STORM

Ramsey MacDonald's deteriorating mental and physical health was making a mockery of his premiership, with incoherent speeches at conferences and in the House of Commons. A timetable was agreed with Baldwin for a handover, and in June 1935, after the King's Silver Jubilee celebrations, Baldwin became Prime Minister. Having a Conservative Prime Minister removed the anomaly of a former Labour (and still National Labour) Prime Minister effectively heading an enormous parliamentary group of Conservative MPs. Baldwin continued with the National Government when he became Prime Minister and after the election later that year, but from the summer of 1935, the Government was a Conservative one in all but name.

  The general election took place in November and although the parties of the National Government lost ground and seats to a recovering Labour Party, the result was still a very comfortable majority for Baldwin. The Labour Party had a new leader to take them into the election after the resignation of the pacifist, George Lansbury. A motion at the Labour Party conference calling for sanctions against Italy after their invasion of Abyssinia at the beginning of October was opposed by Lansbury as he thought sanctions to be a form of "economic warfare". His deputy, Clement Attlee took over and faced a general election almost immediately. The relative success of Labour in the election helped secure Attlee as leader rather than just a caretaker, though this extension was not warmly welcomed by everyone in the Party.

Churchill had also opposed meaningful economic sanctions against Italy as he did not want to antagonise Mussolini or risk a crack in the Stresa front. The Stresa front was a tripartite agreement signed in April 1935 involving Britain, France and Italy which backed-up the Locarno Treaty and reaffirmed the independence of Austria. It also agreed to resist any amendment of the Versailles Treaty in favour of Germany. In truth however, the Stresa front had already been greatly undermined (as had the Versailles treaty) by the signing in June of the Anglo-German naval agreement. The front was effectively dismantled by Italy's invasion of Abyssinia in October. This is another example of Churchill's lack of anti-appeasement credentials in 1935 as he gave tacit approval to Italy's aggression and opposed even economic sanctions against fascist expansion.

Churchill won his seat in the general election held in November 1935, being returned in Epping with an increased majority. In December, Churchill travelled to Spain. A relaxing holiday, initially sailing from Barcelona to Mallorca, saw him spend several weeks in the Mediterranean. Churchill and his wife, Clementine, roamed among the Balearic Islands of Minorca and Mallorca; before Winston sailed to North Africa, including Marrakesh; and spent some time at a hotel in Barcelona on the Spanish mainland. While the idea was to have a peaceful retreat, painting, writing and enjoying some winter sun, Churchill was also trying to get over personal political disappointment. Although he had successfully defended his seat in the British General Election just a few weeks earlier, he had been overlooked for a cabinet position which he thought that he ought to have had. December also saw the end of foreign secretary Hoare, as the Hoare-Lavall Pact had failed to stop the Italian military expansionism in Abyssinia. He was replaced by Anthony Eden, an appointment which left Churchill initially unimpressed.

Baldwin had not chosen Churchill, just as he had also

overlooked him when forming cabinets earlier in the year. This was despite Winston being one of the best known of the Conservative MPs and having had previous cabinet experience under Asquith and Lloyd George as a Liberal and as Baldwin's Conservative Chancellor of the Exchequer for nearly five years in the 1920s. In fact, Baldwin, with some prescience, had shrewdly decided that he could not have Churchill in his cabinet in case the worst should happen, and the country had to look for a new leader. If the British Government's policies failed and Europe was plunged into another major war, Baldwin reasoned that the politicians who had argued against early and large-scale rearmament could not be the ones who waged that war. In those circumstances, Baldwin believed that Churchill could be the only choice as Prime Minister. It was therefore in order not to taint Churchill with the failure of appeasement that Baldwin had excluded him from the cabinet.

However, during the winter of 1935/1936, painting, writing and brooding in the Balearics and North Africa, this level of insurance on behalf of Britain was unknown to Churchill and so began those years, which the future wartime leader himself called, "The Gathering Storm". In this time, Churchill was to be a voice against accommodating Hitler through the policy of appeasement, but he did so from the backbenches, outside the governments of first Baldwin and then Chamberlain, as the second half of the decade continued. While holidaying, Churchill also met and spent time with a person who was to become extremely important to the future wartime leader. At the time of the Churchills' visit in 1935, Alan Hillgarth was the British vice-consul to the Balearics, based at an office in Palma, Mallorca. He lived in a grand finca called Son Torella, twelve miles outside the island's capital.

At the start of the Spanish Civil War, Hillgarth, according to his biographer Duff Hart-Davis "began sending secret reports to the Foreign Office. Without any invitation, he suddenly became an agent of HMG."[1] This started after being returned to the island aboard a British destroyer from a holiday. It seems highly improbable that Hillgarth just started sending reports of his own volition and it is likely that he had been working for British naval intelligence for some time. It is probable that Hillgarth took up the unpaid position of vice-consul in order to make contacts and gain information which would be useful to the British Navy. The strategic position of the Balearics in the Mediterranean was important to control of the area and one which was coveted by Mussolini. Hillgarth was certainly well connected. Not many who had left the navy as a Lieutenant in 1922 could have pulled strings to enable HMS Hood to deliver a large portrait belonging to his wife to their home in Mallorca in the 1930s, still less have a group of petty officers transfer it to his house and hang it.

At the very least, Hillgarth used his position as vice consul to gain valuable information. He saw his role as more than just a functionary and he took it upon himself to entertain in style. He constantly complained about the expenses he was incurring by being vice-consul, including lavish parties at his home on the island. In June 1936, Hillgarth was in London with his family on a holiday and they watched the trooping of the colour ceremony, not from the spectator areas but from the garden of 10 Downing Street as a guest of the Prime Minister, Stanley Baldwin. Hillgarth's biographer is at a loss as to why the Prime Minister should invite him. It seems clear that Hillgarth had other reasons for doing the voluntary work he did in Mallorca when he was meant to be a writer and it is certainly true that he slipped seamlessly into the life of a spy.

Hart-Davis also greatly downplays the contact which Hillgarth had with Churchill in the winter of 1935/1936. The

---
1 Duff Hart-Davis, *Man of War*, p 152.

biographer suggests that this was limited to one lunch as Churchill passed by on the way to catch the boat to Marrakesh. Churchill spent a great deal more time than this at the home of Alan Hillgarth, including staying there and painting. In fact, local Mallorcan newspapers had reported that Hillgarth had met the Churchills as they disembarked at Palma at the start of their visit.[2] Historians David Stafford and Peter Day agree that the Churchills stayed with the Hillgarths for at least a few days during this time. Stafford states that, "Hillgarth put them up for a couple of days"[3] while Day writes that "Churchill spent time at Son Torella relaxing and painting… and deep in discussion about the political developments in Spain."[4] The friendship which began at this time was to become crucial in both the conflicts to follow. Firstly, as Hillgarth was a source of information regarding the progress of the civil war and then officially, as he reported directly to Churchill (when Winston joined Chamberlain's government as First Lord of the Admiralty) from the start of the Second World War.

A convivial host, Hillgarth's position as British vice consul on the island had brought him into contact with many important people. These included Juan March, who financed the Nationalists in the Spanish Civil War and directly aided the Nationalists' leader in that conflict, Francisco Franco. Franco had been made the Commandante General of the Balearics by Prime Minister Azaña to "be far from temptations" and was there from March 1933 until he was recalled (temporally at first) by the new centre-right government in September 1934, shortly before taking command against the miners in Asturias. During his time in Mallorca, Franco was in Hillgarth's company often, an alliance that was to prove important to Hillgarth, Franco and

---

2 *La Vanguardia,* 13 December 1935.
3 David Stafford, *Roosevelt and Churchill Men of Secrets,* p 82.
4 Jimmy Burns, *Papa Spy,* p 22.

Churchill in the second World War. Juan March was a notorious arms and tobacco smuggler and very rich, through this and his shipping and banking interests. He was the richest man in Spain and reputedly the sixth richest in the world.

March's links to Churchill had an inauspicious start when he gave supplies to U-boats of the Central powers from a small island just off Mallorca during World War One. Churchill, as First Lord of the Admiralty, put pressure on the Spanish Government to expropriate the island. While this put an end to that particular avenue of opportunity to make money, March continued to smuggle and supply goods to both sides during the war. Juan March was eventually protected by Primo during the Dictadura, gaining official import licences which effectively legitimised his smuggling, or at least part of it. He diversified into banking and his wealth increased even more. The coming of the second Republic was not welcomed by March and he did his best to destabilize the Spanish currency and economy in order to undermine the new Republic. The feeling of antagonism with the Republic was clearly mutual as he was arrested and imprisoned for financial irregularities. He escaped by bribing a guard and went into exile.

It is clear that Hillgarth was in a good position to update Churchill on the political situation in Spain at this critical time. Hillgarth moved between the islands and the Spanish mainland and was in touch with the fulltime consul in Barcelona. At the time of Churchill's visit, the centre-right government in Madrid was breaking-up under the strain of trying to contain the dictatorial ambition of Gil Robles, leader of the right-wing CEDA, who had the largest number of deputies in the Cortes. Robles saw his opportunity to seize power which had hitherto been denied to him, as the corrupt Radical Party under Lerroux were beset by financial scandals and could clearly not continue. However, President Alcalá-Zamora was rightly distrustful of the intentions of Robles and refused to make him Prime Minister.

As Churchill enjoyed his Spanish holiday, rumours of a possible military coup abounded in Spain as a way out of the political crisis caused by the demise of the Lerroux government. Caught with their fingers in the till once too often, the corrupt politicians of the Radical Party were clearly unfit to govern. Churchill would have been aware of the heightened tension in Barcelona as he stayed in a hotel frequented by local left-wing leaders. A compromise manufactured by Alcalá-Zamora which side-lined Robles was a temporary solution and fresh elections were called, which were scheduled for the beginning of February in 1936. However, before that could occur, the death of George V meant Churchill, by that time in North Africa, had to return to Britain.

Franco, now at the War Ministry in Madrid, had several meetings and conversations during that December 1935 and January 1936 period of uncertainty, about possible military intervention in the government. It was recognised by the Generals that there was too little time for proper planning given the expected resistance that any such coup would face from an organised working class. Franco himself had headed the army's response to the uprising in Asturias just over a year before, where the army had brutally crushed a rebellion by miners and others. Franco had then been hailed as "the saviour of the Republic" but he knew that a military attack on the Republic would likely provoke a united working-class resistance which would be difficult to overcome easily. Franco was also reluctant at the end of 1935 and the beginning of 1936, to be at the beck and call of civilian plotters. Although feted by many right-wing politicians, Franco had little time for them. First and foremost, Franco was a military man who disliked any civilian interference in what he defined himself as his duty to the *Patria*.

Although he was back in Britain and about to be deeply

and personally involved in what became the abdication crisis, Churchill's mind was never far from foreign affairs. As he left the region, the thought of a military dictatorship would not have worried Churchill overly, if the alternative was political chaos, or worse in his mind, the bolshevisation of Spain. The threat from Germany was another matter. Churchill had argued for appeasement of Italy (by not extending sanctions to include oil) following Mussolini's invasion of Abyssinia, precisely on the grounds that the greater threat was from Germany, "we cannot have any anxieties comparable to the anxiety caused by German rearmament."[5]

Back in Mallorca, Hillgarth was concerned at anything which would disturb the business interests of Britain, Spain's largest trading partner in 1936. Elsewhere in Spain, right-wing politicians and army generals were fearful of the elections to come. Unless CEDA could claim a victory without their more centrist erstwhile partners, the discredited Radicals, there might be electoral success for a new grouping.

The Popular Front was an alliance of socialists, communists and left leaning republicans who hoped to take advantage of Spain's electoral laws which favoured broad coalitions. In the previous election in November 1933, a united Right had reaped the benefits of a disunited left to take control. The boot was now on the other foot however as the newly formed Popular Front sought to defeat the fragmented Right. The Popular Front was the product of a changing national and international climate, and an electoral necessity. The PSOE had been shown in the election of the 1933 the folly of isolationism and party purity when it came to Spanish general elections. The intervening two years – known as the Bienio Negro (the two black years) – had shown that no matter how bad a mildly reforming, centre-left government might be, it was infinitely preferrable to a right-wing

---

5 *Hansard*, vol 305, col 368.

one. Added to this was the very real belief that a victory for CEDA in the election could mean the beginning a regime akin to that of the Nazis and thereafter, the death of the Republic. The socialists therefore joined with the centre-left republicans and others, including the numerically small Communist Party, to form an electoral pact to take on the forces of the Right. 1936 also saw a change in tactics from the Comintern in the Soviet Union, with national communist parties in Western European countries now urged to join with other progressives against fascism. The Popular Front movement was to spread to other countries, including successfully in France in just a few months. On the Right, CEDA formed a pact with others, including monarchists and Carlists, to form a "national counter-revolutionary front".[6]

The Spanish Communist Party (PCE) were numerically small in terms of membership, around 30 000 at the beginning of 1936, having been established only in 1920, long after the anarchist movement had taken a firm grip on the Spanish working class and peasantry in many areas, including Catalonia and Aragon. The PCE therefore struggled to gain mass appeal on the Left, squeezed between the anarchist and syndicalist FAI/CNT on the one side and the party machine of the organised socialist party and their trade union, the PSOE/UGT on the other.

As with all communist parties of their type in Europe at the time, the PCE took their "line" from Moscow, unlike another Marxist group, the numerically small POUM (*Partido Obrero de Unificación Marxista*) the Workers' Party of Marxist Unification. Often called Trotskyist (although disowned by Trotsky for merging with another party) this was the grouping whose militia

---

6 The Carlists were supporters of another branch of the monarchy who had taken part in civil wars and uprisings in Spain in the 19th century in support of their cause. By the 1930s, they were opposed to the Republic and centred in Navarre. They were extremely religious and by this time also paramilitary, with officers trained in Italy by Mussolini.

George Orwell joined when he went to fight for the Republic in the Spanish Civil War. Politics in Spain in the 1930s were complicated, especially among the groupings and factions on the Left. It is impossible to understand the period fully without an appreciation of this and some grasp of the beliefs, strategies and conflict that existed. Although Churchill could often show great command of detail in many areas, including military ones, his lack of appreciation and understanding of the make-up of the Left led him to make mistakes in his approach to Spain.

January 1936 saw the end of George V's reign in Britain and the demise of the centre-right government of the Spanish Republic. There was uncertainty over who would succeed the latter. President Alcalá-Zamora's insistence on calling new elections meant that not just the governance but the entire future direction of Spain was in the balance. Franco was not alone in preferring a "wait and see" policy towards events. For Churchill, there was no doubt about the succession in Britain, he wrote in typically sycophantic, romantic hyperbole to the new King, Edward VIII, "Your Majesty's name shall shine in history as the bravest and best beloved of all the sovereigns who have worn the Island Crown." He was seldom more wrong.

5
THE ELECTORAL VICTORY OF THE POPULAR FRONT

In February 1936, Spain held an election to its parliament, the Cortes. In a polarised country, there were two main blocks: on the right there was CEDA, led by Gil Robles, an admirer of Hitler who sought to emulate the German leader's tactics of using the mechanism of democracy in order to destroy it; on the left was the Popular Front, led by Manuel Azaña, a centre left, anti-clerical republican of the Republican Left Party (*Izquierda Republicana*). The Popular Front included the numerically superior *Partido Socialista Obrero Espanol* (PSOE - Spain's socialist party); regional/national left parties and the small Spanish Communist Party, PCE. It would be the last free election in Spain for forty years.

The Spanish electoral system was designed to encourage broad coalitions. If parties could get together in electoral pacts, then the seats they obtained would far outweigh the proportion of votes for each of the parties individually. In 1933, CEDA – itself a grouping of right-wing Catholics and proto-fascists – had worked with other right wing and centre-right parties to gain a victory over the disunited left. By 1936 however, the Radical Republican party of Lerroux, CEDA's main partner, had been discredited due to corruption scandals and criminal activities. Gil Robles could not find enough willing partners to create the broad coalition which might have brought electoral success, caused in part by his increasingly pro-Nazi rhetoric.

In contrast, the left had learned their lesson and were willing to work together to defeat the right. They were aware that there was a danger of Spain following Germany's lead if Robles became Prime Minister. The President, Alcalá-Zamora, a conservative supporter of the Republic, had managed to thwart Robles' ambitions so far and had arranged for the election rather than give Robles power, only too aware of the fate of Germany. All recognised that if Robles won this time, it would be difficult to legally deny Robles the Premiership. The stakes could not have been higher.

By the middle of January 1936, an agreement had been reached by almost all of the left and progressive parties to fight the election under a common programme as the Popular Front. Their manifesto was modest: reversing most of the changes brought in during the Bienio Negro immediately previous, which itself had largely been a reversal of the reforms of the centre-left first government of the second republic that had been in power for over two years from 1931.

The Popular Front had also been made possible by the decision of the Spanish communists, the *Partido Comunista de España* (PCE) to join other parties committed to anti-fascism. In fact, the communists were very much the junior partners in the Spanish Popular Front and were dwarfed by the socialists of the PSOE. The ambitions of the communists were modest and they were generally less radical than many others on the left, allowing some to quip 'Vote communist and save Spain from Marxism.' The Popular Front also contained the Republican Left led by Azaña and the Republican Union led by Barrio. The left Catalan parties, ERC, USC and AC were prominent members too.

Although not formally part of the Popular Front, the anarchists still played a part in its support. In many parts of Spain, including Catalonia, anarchism was very popular among both the working class and the peasants. The anarchist CNT was a major trade union in large areas and had a huge membership.

The Electoral Victory of the Popular Front

The promise of the Popular Front to give an amnesty to the political prisoners of the failed 1934 Asturias uprising ensured the support of most anarchists at the ballot box and urged on by Durruti among others, the Popular Front gained the votes of those who would otherwise have abstained.

CEDA were financed for the election by Juan March (See Chapter 4) to a level which could never have been matched by the left. This paid for 50 million CEDA leaflets, distributed to every part of Spain possible, by lorry and even by aeroplane. CEDA propaganda depicted the choice in the election as between order and chaos. They appealed to their key groups of supporters, especially the religious. They forecast looting of private property and even the nationalisation of women unless people backed them. They lacked coalition partners however and their "national counter revolutionary front" consisted of themselves along with Alfonsine monarchists and Carlists.

The Popular Front's electoral campaign concentrated on preventing fascism and relied on the unease that had built up among some moderates about the intentions of CEDA. In truth however, by 1936, there was little support for the centre parties remaining in Spain. Most people were committed to one side or the other and both of these groupings were pulling further apart. The election campaign was marred by violence, as had happened just over two years earlier, with over forty killed, most of them on the left.

Polls opened on the 16th February with both sides seemingly confident of victory. The results were to be disputed later (by Franco among others) but in fact if they were generally fair and any corruption in the first round of voting favoured the right. Even the monarchist newspaper ABC declared that the poll was fair, "everyone voted as they wanted to, in absolute liberty" as it was confident of a CEDA victory. The results came in over the next few days and showed a clear victory, in seats at least, for the Popular Front.

In August 1936, Churchill talked about the result of the election, but was misinformed as to the figures. He believed that most people in Spain were on the side of the Nationalists in the civil war (this was certainly untrue) and tried to use incorrect totals from the February election to justify this assertion. He said that four and a half million had voted for various Conservative parties of the Right and Centre against four and a quarter million who voted for the Left. Although there are disputes about the figures, all modern historians show a majority of votes for the Popular Front. Looking at the February election alone (rerun elections up to May saw more of a vote for Popular Front), the margin of victory may have been as small as 75,000 votes, though some show a slightly larger figure.

If the results of the elections were close in terms of votes, with a small majority for the Popular Front, the Spanish electoral system translated this into a sizeable majority in the Cortes in terms of seats. The PSOE emerged as the largest single party, (99 seats) with their Popular Front allies, Azaña's new party, *Izquierda Republicana* (Republican Left) who came back from the near annihilation of the centre-left in 1933 to have 87 seats, just one short of the CEDA total. The Republican Union had 37. The Left Catalan parties had a total of 30. The PCE had 17 seats. The big losers were the discredited Radical Republicans, with Lerroux losing his seat. Many of their votes went to CEDA or Centre parties. Compared to 1933, the Right increased their votes by around ¾ of a million, however the Left increased theirs by over a million. This was a demonstration of the increasing polarisation of Spanish politics, even though the programme of the Popular Front was mild. In the end, the Popular Front gained at least 267 of the 473 seats, however by May, after reruns, this had risen to 285; compared to 146 for the Right (National) bloc (131 by May).

The Electoral Victory of the Popular Front

Not everyone was prepared to accept the results of the election, despite their fairness. Franco contacted the head of the Civil Guard to try to persuade him to commit his men to backing a coup. He contacted sympathetic officers around the country to be prepared for action and tried to have martial law imposed over all of Spain. Franco, Gil Robles and others tried to get the interim government to refuse to hand over power to the Popular Front and offered the support of the army to help them in their stance. To their credit, the outgoing Government recognised the legitimacy of the election outcome and turned down offers to help them remain in power by force, transferring the governance of Spain to the Popular Front. They did not however pass on any note of the proposed treachery of Franco and others.

There were several reruns of elections in different parts of the country in the following months, nearly all of which led to increased representation for the Popular Front (one of the reasons for the disparity in figures between different commentators). There have been allegations that some of these secondary elections were unfair and influenced by the now Popular Front regime, however even if this was the case, the overall outcome was unchanged and any low-level corruption was unlikely to have matched the machinations of the right who had tried to manipulate the vote, especially in rural areas, in the February election. On the announcement of the results, the Left took to the streets to celebrate while many on the Right began to plot their next move. Political violence increased, which of course suited the agenda of those who said that Spain was not capable of democracy and that it needed strong, military backed leadership instead. The election of the Popular Front meant that the fuse for the civil war had been lit.

Though momentarily captured by the election in Spain and some of the political violence which followed the result, Europe's attention was soon grabbed by Hitler's troops marching into the Rhineland, in contravention of both the Versailles and Locarno treaties. The movement of troops by Hitler was a calculated risk. He knew that Germany was not in a position to adequately counter any military response from France or Britain, but he calculated that they would not do so. Hitler was proved correct as Britain in particular was not going to go to war over the Germans moving troops about 'in their own back garden'. Any complaint about contravention of the Treaty of Versailles was already a busted flush. In the previous year, Britain and Germany had signed the Anglo-German naval pact which allowed Germany to build up its navy, in direct contravention of the Treaty. 1935 had also seen the introduction of military service, meaning that Germany would have an army larger than the 100 000 men allowed by the Versailles Treaty; and then the announcement by Germany that it had created its own air force, again in contravention of Versailles, and with devastating consequences in Spain just a short time later.

Churchill, reflecting on these breaches later, said "Once Hitler's Germany had been allowed to rearm without interference by the Allies… a second World War was almost certain."[1] The response of the British and French governments was better than Hitler could have wished for. Baldwin, as Prime Minister, and others in the British Government made it clear to the French that Britain was not prepared to do anything which could result in war and urged France not to do so either. There is little doubt that the French army at that time could have moved into the Rhineland and forced Hitler to retreat, however they were reluctant to act. Although they were supported by the "Little Entente" of smaller countries, including Czechoslovakia, the French were worried that internal division would prove intolerable if they acted without Britain. The result was inaction: strong words but nothing which Hitler could not easily withstand. This was the

---
1 Winston Churchill, T*he Gathering Storm*, p 170.

final nail in the coffin of the League of Nations and the notion of collective security. Badly damaged by the lack of effective sanctions against either Japan or Italy following invasions of Manchuria and Abyssinia respectively, the League already looked weak. Britain was duty bound to take action against a breach of Versailles and to come to the aid of France if they acted against such a breach. Since Britain itself had aided Hitler's wilful ignoring of the naval and army limitations placed on Germany by Versailles, it should have come as no surprise that Baldwin and his Government would not act this time. The British leaders always cited the pacifist mood of the country, still reeling from the first World War. However, in doing so, they often ignored the corollary of this which was that in place of war, peace had to be maintained – and aggressors deterred – by collective security. Baldwin in 1936 and Chamberlain after him, both failed to see the folly of trying to maintain peace without the collective strength of the peaceful nations.

    Churchill blamed the Rhineland crisis for his exclusion from a new committee to oversee the co-ordination of defence. He believed that it was the militarisation of the Rhineland that meant that he could not be seen to be promoted to a military linked position as, "Hitler would not like it".[2] In fact Churchill was being given unprecedented access to the Admiralty and classified documents, with the approval of the First Sea Lord. Much has been made about secrets being courageously passed on to Churchill so that he could maintain his crusade against the Government's policy of appeasement, but in truth, much of the information he used to mount his attacks on first Baldwin and then Chamberlain's policies, was handed to him by officials quite openly. Throughout the spring and early summer of 1936, Churchill railed against the increasing militarisation of Germany. He bemoaned the amount spent on the German navy

---

2 Winston Churchill, *The Gathering Storm*, p 180.

and compared this unfavourably with spending in Britain. In May, Churchill asked what all the German military spending was for, "Certainly it is not all for fun. Something quite extraordinary is afoot. All the signals are set for danger."[3] All of which makes his reaction to German military aggression in Spain just a few months later even more contradictory to his supposed anti-appeasement stance and opposition to German militarism.

The Popular Front Government in Spain in the spring of 1936 was setting about implementing its relatively modest programme of reform. Alcalá-Zamora was removed as President and Azaña took his place at the beginning of April. At the start of May, Azaña appointed Casares Quiroga as Prime Minister (the title was actually President of the Council of Ministers, but it was the equivalent of Prime Minister). Spain was again engulfed in a wave of political murders, with the far-right Falange in particular, openly at war with anyone remotely left wing. Booksellers, judges, journalists and army captains all fell victim to the Falange death squads. To combat this, the communists and the socialists each set up their own paramilitary organisations and soon tit-for-tat killings were common. This played into the hands of those who wanted an excuse to forcibly enter the political arena to "restore order" and of course, this is exactly the environment that the Falange wished to create.

It was against this background that many of the generals in the Spanish army were plotting to bring down the elected government. In truth, the plotting had begun even before the handover of power, as we have seen, when some were prepared to use the army to prevent the inauguration of the Popular Front. The head of the plotters was General Mola, who began organising for a military take over almost immediately following the announcement of the election results. In Morocco in March, he prepared the troops there for a future rising. Summoned

---

3 Winston Churchill, *Step by Step*, p 16.

back to the peninsula, Mola met in Madrid with several other generals, including Franco, before going to his new posting in Pamplona. The capital of the Navarre region was the perfect place for him as it was the stronghold of the Carlists and their military wing, the *requetes*, though this had not been the intention of the Government when placing him there. Mola was to be the Director of firstly a conspiracy and then a coup, but the Generals agreed that although Mola would be in charge of the plans, at the head of conspiracy should be the exiled Sanjurjo, who was in Portugal.

Franco was geographically sidelined by the Popular Front Government (along with other generals thought to be hostile to the Republic) by being posted as far from the centre of action as possible and arrived in the Canary islands in March 1936. He flirted with standing in one of the re-run elections for the Cortes but eventually withdrew. Franco saw being sent to the Canaries as another slight from Azaña and added it to his list of personal grievances against the man who would become President weeks later. On the mainland, Mola continued plotting, involving both civilian and military people for what was expected to be a relatively swift takeover of power. Different Generals were given areas that they were to take control of, but Franco dithered over whether to commit himself or not. Franco could not have borne the humiliation that he would have suffered if the coup was a flop and he wanted to be sure as possible of likely success before finally pledging himself. Mola was determined that the coup would go ahead with or without Franco and sent out general orders to the conspirators with detailed plans for a future rising.

At the beginning of July, Franco was still not committed to the coup. In Mola's plan, Franco was to make the short flight from the Canary Islands to Spanish Morocco and there take charge of the army of Africa, by far the best troops in the Spanish army. The high regard in which Franco was held by the Moroccan troops, both *regulares* and *legionnaires*, made his participation in the coup important to Mola. There was very little chance of success without the backing of the Army of Africa and Franco was considered the best (though by no means the only) person to lead it. Franco was also well respected by many of the officers throughout the army, from his time in charge of the Military Academy and when he was Chief of Staff and his participation in the coup may well persuade some other army officers to join it. Sanjurjo still did not trust him after his refusal firstly to join the attempted coup in 1932 and then to defend Sanjurjo at his trial. However, assured that Franco would seek only the Governorship of Morocco in return, he acknowledged that the rising had more chance of success with Franco than without, if Franco could be persuaded to join the other rebel Generals. The stage was set for another act of violent regime change in Spain to take place in July 1936, against the backdrop of an increasing volatile Europe.

6
THE BLONDES IN THE DRAGON RAPIDE

In the re-writing of history by Franco and his apologists that followed the attempted coup and the subsequent Civil War, it was a political murder which sparked the rising. Calvo Sotelo was one of the most prominent figures on the right of Spanish politics, having served as Finance Minister under Miguel Primo de Rivera in the 1920s and subsequently leader of the *Renovacion Espanola* (his move to join the Falange was blocked by Jose Antonio Primo de Rivera – Miguel's son - as he regarded Calvo Sotelo as a potential leadership rival). On 12th July 1936, a Falange death squad had murdered an Assault Guard officer because of his left-wing sympathies. Some of his comrades sought immediate revenge, trying first to find Gil Robles (who was on holiday) and then seizing and killing Calvo Sotelo before dumping his body. The assassination caused outrage among the right, while many on the left feared the backlash this would bring and openly called for the government to arm the workers. This did not however cause the attempted coup by the Generals, as there had been months of careful planning and the date was set for the 18th July. What it did do however was to cement Franco's support for, and participation in, that rising. Right up to that point, Franco had swithered, and contingency had been made for his exclusion, when news of Calvo Sotelo's death led him to contact Mola to confirm his involvement. The other result of the death of Sotelo for Franco, although he would not have fully realised it at the time, was to remove a potential rival for the leadership of the Right. If Sanjurjo was to be the military supremo and likely Head of State in the event of a successful coup, Calvo Sotelo would have been the leading contender (along with the imprisoned Jose Antonio Primo de Rivera) as the political head. The timely death of rivals was to be a significant feature of Franco's rise to leadership.

    Even before anything started in Spain, events involving Britain played an important part in Franco's role in the coup. The plotters in Spain had contacts and friends among intelligence, political and aristocratic circles in London. One of the chief go-betweens was Luis Bolin, a journalist for the monarchist ABC newspaper in Spain, who would go on to become Franco's press chief during the Civil War. He made friends with Douglas Jerrold, a British intelligence agent and a right-wing Catholic, editor of the *London Review*. Jerrold desired to see Britain ruled by a benign dictator, more like Mussolini than Hitler. Bolin asked Jerrold if he could put him in contact with someone who could arrange for a plane and pilot. Jerrold had no hesitation in recommending Hugh Pollard, who had been in British intelligence for decades. Pollard had spread misinformation and propaganda in the first World War and in Ireland. In the latter, he was involved in a scandal when he faked an IRA attack and had published photographs which were proved to be false. He had also taken part in live and dangerous operations and was fluent in Spanish from his time as a mercenary and adventurer in Mexico many years previously. His political views were, in his own words, "extreme right". Bolin had asked for "a reliable man and two platinum blondes to deflect attention from their real purpose."[1] Pollard was that man and when tasked later with getting the girls, he said he could. These conspirators secured a pilot and a twin-engine Dragon Rapide plane (the whole enterprise was well financed by Juan March). Pollard asked his 19-year-old daughter Diana and her friend Dorothy to come

---

1 Peter Day, *Franco's Friends*, p 4.

with him. The actual purpose of the flight was to collect Franco from the Canary Islands and take him to Morocco at the start of the coup.

The plane took off from Croydon airport on 11th July, notably before the assassination of Calvo Sotelo and conclusive proof that the coup going ahead at this time had nothing to do with his murder. The plane contained the pilot (Cecil Bebb), Luis Bolin, Hugh Pollard, his daughter Diana, her friend Dorothy and a radio operator. The flight was to take them to the Canary Islands via Bordeaux, Lisbon, Casablanca and Spanish Morocco. In Bordeaux they picked up the Marques de Morito and headed for Lisbon. It was in the Portuguese capital that their plans changed twice. Firstly, it was decided that the coup could no longer wait for Franco to commit and that they should bring Sanjurjo on the plane to Spain once the coup started. Then Calvo Sotelo was killed and the plotters were unsure of their next move. According to his daughter, it was Pollard who said that they should continue to fly to Casablanca. It was agreed to go there and await developments. If not needed, they would all fly home on 31st July. In Casablanca, word came through that Franco had now agreed to join the coup, Luis Bolin remained in Casablanca as the plane with Bebb, Pollard, Diana and Dorothy on board (the drunken radio operator had been sent home) flew to Port Juby in Spanish Morocco, planning to refuel before flying on to the Canaries. The Spanish authorities however were suspicious of the of the plans. Diana Pollard later related what happened next:

"We didn't waste one minute. We got on the plane and headed for Gran Canaria. As soon as we left they sent up an army plane to catch us because the message from Gran Canaria was to stop us. But we were faster so we landed in Las Palmas and they impounded the aeroplane."[2]

---

[2] Interview with Diana Pollard by the Imperial War Museum, in Peter Day, *Franco's Friends*.

On the 14th July, when the plane landed, Franco was in Tenerife and not able to go to Gran Canaria without permission (he had already requested and been refused). Hugh Pollard and his party escaped surveillance and managed to get a boat to Tenerife to meet Franco and pass on documents Pollard was carrying from the conspirators. At this point, another timely death came to Franco's aid. The military commander of Gran Canaria, General Balmes, accidently shot himself meaning Franco could legitimately travel for his funeral. Although Balmes shooting himself in the stomach by accident on the firing range was extremely fortuitous for Franco and the coup as a whole, there is no actual evidence that the death was anything more sinister, however doubts remain. Balmes is believed to have resisted overtures to join the coup and his death not only gave Franco a reason to return to Gran Canaria but also helped to ensure that the island would fall to the rebels. Franco travelled on an overnight boat back to Gran Canaria with a small band of supporters. Pollard and the two women were on the same boat. The coup was due to begin on the 18th of July, as planned by Mola. However, some of the plotters in Morocco believed they were about to be uncovered and possibly arrested, so they moved earlier and begun the uprising on the evening of the 17th. They secured the main towns in the colony and awaited the arrival of Franco. Bebb piloted the plane back across to Africa, with Franco on board, arriving in Casablanca, where they picked up Luis Bolin. On the morning of the 19th they flew to Spanish Morocco, where Franco would take over as leader of the Army of Africa. Bebb was then asked to fly to Lisbon with Bolin on board to take Sanjurjo to Spain and then fly onwards to Rome with Bolin to seek help from Mussolini. Franco gave Bolin a note asking for aeroplanes from Britain, Germany or Italy. The Dragon Rapide took off for the Portuguese capital once more. Hugh Pollard, with Diana and Dorothy remained in Gran Canaria throughout all of this and returned to Britain a few weeks later. After the war, Bebb, Pollard, Diana and Dorothy were all given medals by Franco for their part in the coup and his rise to leadership.

On the Spanish mainland, the coup met with mixed success. Initially on the morning of the 18th, Prime Minister Quiroga had announced that the uprising was limited to the Protectorate of Morocco and that an anti-republican movement on the mainland had been defeated by swift action. Unfortunately, the action he referred to was that of General Quiepo de llano in the South of Spain, who Quiroga believed had secured the region for the Republic when he had done the exact opposite and had seized it for the conspirators. Quiepo was a relative of Alcalá-Zamora and believed to be a strong supporter of the Republic, but he had despised the way Alcalá-Zamora was treated when losing the Presidency and had joined the conspiracy. He was able to capture Seville despite working class resistance and then set about murdering political opponents and others in the most brutal and merciless fashion. The trade unions recognised the threat from the attempted coup immediately and demanded that Quiroga arm the workers. In many places the allegiance of the armed Civil Guard and local army garrisons was not fixed. Where armed and aggressive working-class groups showed they were prepared to storm barracks and take action themselves, the Civil Guards or soldiers often sided with the Republic. Where this was not the case, often due to a lack of arms or because a civic leader had called for caution, the military or paramilitary force, persuaded by their officers, went over to the side of the Generals.

Mola had perhaps the easiest posting on the mainland as Pamplona was the Carlist stronghold and crowds of people there heralded the coup as if it was a religious festival, shouting "Christ the King" and marching in support of the rising. Elsewhere in Spain, most of the civilian population was against the coup and crucially so were large parts of the armed forces. Madrid, Barcelona, Valencia and Malaga were all held for the Republic through a mixture of loyal troops, Assault Guards and armed workers. Cadiz was won for Rising when reinforcements from the Army of Africa were brought over by a destroyer. This was part of the plan for the plotters. Once Morocco was secured, the best and perhaps only really reliable troops – the Army of Africa – were to be brought over the short crossing from North Africa to mainland Spain. The plan failed however due to the rank-and-file sailors who mostly stayed loyal to the republic, often killing their officers who rebelled, and secured around three quarters of the Spanish navy for the Government (even the destroyer which had landed the troops in Cadiz was won back over to the Republic by the ordinary sailors). This left most of the Army of Africa stranded in Morocco and was a major blow to any hopes of a quick victory for the Generals.

Quiroga was being overwhelmed by events and refused to arm the workers, even saying that anyone who did so would be shot. He did not want the country sliding further into chaos but this delay almost certainly meant that the coup was not crushed. If he had issued an order to local officials in mainland Spain to arm those loyal to the Republic, there is no doubt that many areas would not have gone over to the rebellion and perhaps the whole coup on the mainland could have been defeated. Quiroga resigned in the early hours of the 19th and Azaña appointed Martinez Barrio Prime Minister. Martinez Barrio formed a government made up only of Republicans and not any of the left-wing elements of the Popular Front as his strategy was to reach out to the Generals and find a compromise. However, when he spoke to Mola by telephone, Mola rejected the proposal, pointing out that if they were to compromise, they would both be betraying their principles and supporters. The news of an attempt to accommodate the traitorous Generals brought furious protests from workers in Madrid and Martinez Barrio was forced to step down after only a few hours in the job. Azaña turned to another friend, a university professor named Jose Giral, to take on the role of Prime Minister. He did so and recognised what was happening for what it was. He disbanded the army and gave instructions to arm the workers.

Even when writing much later and with the benefit of hindsight, Churchill misrepresented what had happened in July 1936 in Spain. As was so often the case, he allowed his own prejudices to obscure the facts.

"At the end of 1936, the increasing degeneration of the Parliamentary regime in Spain, and the growing strength of the movements for a Communist, or alternatively an anarchist revolution led to a military revolt which had long been preparing."[3]

The "long been preparing" part was correct and Churchill will have been aware of it at the time, without necessarily knowing all the detail. It contradicts the thrust of his statement though, that the military revolt was in response to an imminent threat. The threat for Churchill was of course a Communist revolution. This is despite the numerical inferiority of the Communists in Spain at this time and their political position in 1936 which was to work with the bourgeois democratic forces against fascism and to counter any revolutionary movements. Churchill is closer to the mark with his comment about anarchism, however it was the military rising which provoked an anarchist revolution (which took hold in the early part of the Civil War in Catalonia, Aragon and elsewhere). In fact, it was the communists who quelled this revolution and were firmly in the "war" camp of the "war or revolution" debate among the left in Spain in as the Civil War

---

3 Winston Churchill, *The Gathering Storm*, p 191 - though much of it and the next quote is lifted from an article Churchill wrote in early August 1936 and later republished in *Step by Step* – see chapter 7.

took hold in 1936.

Churchill continued, "A perfect reproduction of the Kerensky period in Russia was taking place in Spain. But the strength of Spain had not been shattered by a foreign war. The army still maintained a measure of cohesion. Side by side with the Communist conspiracy there was elaborated in secret a deep military counterplot. Neither side could claim with justice the title-deeds of legality."[4]

This is about as gross a misrepresentation of the events of 1936 as it would be possible to imagine. The analogy with Russia in 1917 does not stand scrutiny. The victory of the Popular Front in February was not the equivalent of the downfall of the Romanov dynasty in the February revolution. The abdication of the Spanish monarch had not only happened five years before, but the country had had several free and fair elections since then. The government of the Popular Front was by no means provisional, in the way that Kerensky's had been. Stating that the army still maintained a measure of cohesion is to praise it, not for being the force of stability in backing the legal government but for doing the exact opposite. The notion that there was a Communist conspiracy prior to the attempted military coup is a complete fabrication and any level of understanding of the politics of Spain in 1936 would show this to be the case. Finally, it is to be lamented that Churchill, even in retrospect, could not acknowledge the legitimacy of the elected Government. His hatred of communism was greater than any love he had for democracy.

As it became clear that the coup had failed and a Civil War began to develop, the two sides held various advantages over each other. In addition to around three-quarters of the navy, almost all of the small Spanish Airforce remained loyal. The Republic also had control of most of the major cities,

---

4 Winston Churchill, *The Gathering Storm*, p 191.

manufacturing and mining areas and the country's gold reserves. The Nationalists (as Franco and Mola's side came to be known as) had the 40 000 strong Army of Africa, although much of it was stranded in Morocco. They had secured the *Regularies* and Moroccan reinforcements from tribespeople by telling them that the Republic wanted to abolish Allah. Each side had around 50 000 men from the peninsular army, with the paramilitary Assault Guards, Civil Guards and *carabineros* split slightly in favour of the Republic (around 33 000 to 30 000). With forces split fairly evenly but more resources in the hands of the Republic, a long war seemed inevitable, with the Nationalists unlikely to be able to win. The decisive difference came from abroad.

The Spanish Civil War started as a failed military coup but must be seen in the context of wider European events. The Popular Fronts that came to power in Spain and then France in 1936, did so because of the perceived threat to democracy from fascism. Italy and Germany had already fallen and many, not just those on the left, saw the real danger from not working together to combat similar forces in their own countries. The military muscles of Italy and Germany were being flexed in Abyssinia and the Rhineland respectively, and in their attitudes to the League of Nations and international treaties. In a similar way, their ideologies had found a degree of adherence in many countries scarred by the ravages of the depression. In Spain, although the avowedly fascist Falange had minimal support, the much cleverer Gil Robles saw himself as a potential Spanish Hitler and came close to winning an election which would have put his hands on the levers of power of the Spanish state. Tensions were still high following the election, but a disastrous regime had been avoided when the Popular Front won a comfortable majority of seats and began to implement its modest programme of social and economic reform. Political murders continued, in a similar way to events in France at the time, and there were pressures on the Spanish Government from both left and right. Spain in 1936 was part of the dwindling family of democracies in Europe. The threat to this came from the attempted coup of the Generals. Neither the British Government, following a policy of appeasement, nor Churchill, who publicly opposed the policy, could see the events in Spain for what they were.

The government in Britain, as we shall see, outwardly acted in a manner consistent with their general European policy of the time of not taking any action which could be seen as hostile to Hitler or Mussolini. The reaction can be seen as part of the wider policy of appeasement, however there are many who believe that Britain went much further than this and actively encouraged and supported the coup and subsequently the Nationalist side in the Civil war which followed. The involvement of two British intelligence agents in the plotting of the coup and the crucial role they played in moving Franco to Morocco to lead the Army of Africa cannot be ignored. It has never been established conclusively whether or not this was an official action. British military intelligence was well practised in acts which were plausibly deniable and in many ways the subterfuge involved was very similar to other actions involving Hugh Pollard. The blondes in the Dragon Rapide may have been a rogue operation but at the very least British intelligence knew of it, allowed two of their own to be involved and did nothing to prevent it.

7
POSITION NO. 1: CHURCHILL BACKS THE NATIONALISTS

During the second World War, Churchill told the Duke of Alba (Franco's representative in Britain, see chapter 8) that when the Spanish Civil War first started, "I was one of your supporters."[1] Although he had reason to try to sweettalk the Duke of Alba at the time of the lunch in December 1940, there is little doubt that Churchill's first thought in the summer of 1936 was to see a victory for the Nationalists and a defeat for the Republic. Writing with hindsight after the second world war, Churchill said that of the Spanish Civil War, "In this quarrel I was neutral."[2] However, this was not the case. Whatever Churchill was saying in public about being neutral, he was making his personal views quite clear in private. In October 1937, Brigadier Packenham-Walsh visited Churchill at Chartwell and wrote in his diary an account of a conversation on the Spanish Civil War, "Winston says at heart he is for Franco."[3]

Churchill wrote about the failed coup and the Civil War which was now starting, on 10th August 1936 in a piece called "The Spanish Tragedy". In this he said of the reason for the current events in Spain, "the passions of a poverty stricken and backward

---

[1] Spanish Ministry of Foreign Affairs, quoted in Richard Wigg, *Churchill and Spain: The survival of the Franco regime 1940–1945*, p 26.
[2] Winston Churchill, *The Gathering Storm*, p 192.
[3] Packenham-Walsh Diary, 17/10/37, in Robert Rhodes James, *Winston S. Churchill: His Complete Speeches V-III*, pp 799–800.

proletariat demand the overthrow of Church, State and property, and the inauguration of a Communist Regime."[4] This was so far removed from the actual events leading up to the outbreak of the civil war in Spain as to be almost incomprehensible and yet it was disinformation such as this spread by Churchill which prevented many people learning the truth about Spain at the time. It is also in sharp contrast to how he described the motivation and actions of the Nationalist side, "patriotic, religious and bourgeois forces, under the leadership of the army, and sustained by the countryside in many provinces, are marching to re-establish order by setting up a military dictatorship."[5] Even this last part was no criticism of the Nationalists, Churchill remember was an admirer of Mussolini and went on the say, "All the national and martial forces in Spain have been profoundly stirred by the rise of Italy under Mussolini to Imperial power in the Mediterranean. Italian methods are a guide."[6]

With Italy as a model and emulating Mussolini, the Nationalists were to create a new Spain. "The old Spain fell with the monarchy"[7] which was much lamented by Churchill, as we have seen. "The Parliamentary constitution has led to a chaos of blood and fire. Who will make the New Spain and in what form?"[8] Churchill posed his question and gave two possible answers, though professing not to like either, (he had already dismissed Parliamentary democracy, despite Spain being one) he clearly favoured one outcome more than the other. "A revived Fascist Spain in closest sympathy with Italy and Germany is one kind of disaster. A Communist Spain spreading its snaky tentacles through Portugal and France is another, and many will think

---

4 Winston Churchill, *Step by Step*, p 38.
5 *Ibid*. p 38.
6 *Ibid*. p 40.
7 *Ibid*. p 40.
8 *Ibid*. p 40.

Position No. 1: Churchill backs the Nationalists

the worse."[9] It is interesting to note that Spain being ruled by a military dictatorship was not the problem per se, it was that the country might then be closer to Italy and – especially – Germany. A brutal military regime, persecuting opponents was permissible and only became a problem if it allied with Germany. This is exactly the policy that Churchill then pursued when in power as Prime Minister in the 1940s (see Chapter 15 onwards).

Churchill had another motive in writing as he did. When the Generals rose against the Republic, it seemed that another democracy was under threat, which was concerning to most people in Britain. There was a natural reaction to support the Republic against the militarism and almost certain dictatorship that would follow a Nationalist victory. An outpouring of sympathy in Britain (and elsewhere) saw organisations set up to raise funds for charities supporting relief efforts in Spain and groups such as The Scottish Ambulance Unit sent very practical aid. Although difficult to judge absolutely, it seems clear that the majority of people in Britain wanted to see the Nationalists defeated, though without Britain getting involved militarily. This intensified as the Nationalists' deliberate bombing of civilians, using German and Italian air forces as well as shelling, became impossible to deny.

Faced with this public sympathy for the Republic, Churchill wanted to reframe the Civil War as between the forces of military order and communist chaos. In doing this, he hoped to steer British public opinion away from sympathy with the Republic towards neutrality. He did so through disinformation and wilful ignorance of the political picture. This was demonstrated again in his article quoted above when he expanded upon his description of the conflict as being between two new Spains:

"If it were a question of the Old Spain against a New

---

9 Ibid. p 40.

Spain, between the faith, traditions and culture of the past and the appetites and hopes of the future, it would probably go hard with the so called 'rebels'. But this is not the issue. Two new Spains are struggling for mastery. Two antagonistic modern systems are in mortal grapple. Fascism confronts Communism. The spirit and prowess of Mussolini and of Hitler strive with those of Trotsky and Bela Kun."[10]

There is no doubt that the Nationalist side were communing with not just the spirit and prowess of Mussolini and Hitler, but the actual leaders themselves. Both Italy and Germany had parts of their armed forces in Spain on the Nationalist side, so that half of Churchill's equation was completely correct. The other part however was completely wrong, in both its general thrust - that the Republican side in August 1936 were communist - and in its detail, the comical inclusion of the bogeymen, Trotsky and Kun. The Republican Government in August 1936 was led by the Republican Prime Minister, Jose Giral, under President Azaña of the same party. Both were middle class, centre left politicians and very far removed from being communists. Furthermore, Giral's Cabinet throughout August was comprised of only centre left Republicans. There were no socialists in it, never mind communists.

Churchill's choice of Trotsky and Kun is also incorrect. At this time, Trotsky, who had served as Foreign Minister for the Bolsheviks in the very early days following the 1917 October revolution in Russia, and who had then led the successful Red Army in the Russian civil war, was in exile. Having been expelled from the Soviet Union in 1929, Trotsky was currently in Norway and played very little part, in person or in representation, in the machinations of the Spanish Left. One group in Spain at the time who were called Trotskyist were the *Partido Obrero de Unificación Marxista* (POUM). Trotsky himself had fallen

---

10 *Ibid.* p 39-40.

Position No. 1: Churchill backs the Nationalists

out with the *Izquierda Communista de España* (ICE) known as the Trotskyist Left of Spain when they had merged with the Workers and Peasants Bloc (BOC) to form the POUM in 1935. The POUM were regarded as a Trotskyist Party though and they opposed Stalinism in the Soviet Union. The POUM were part of the Popular Front and had one seat in the Cortes from the 1936 election. Although their membership grew in 1936, it was never more than 70 000. Therefore, suggesting that the communists were channelling Trotsky was wrong on an international level and in a Spanish context, where the official communist party, the PCE, despised Trotsky and the POUM.

Churchill's other choice of bogeyman, Bela Kun, is also strange. Kun was a Hungarian communist who had been the Foreign Minister (but de facto leader) of the short-lived Hungarian Soviet Republic which lasted from March 1919 until August that year, when it fell to Romanian and other allied forces as well as internal pressures. Since then, Kun had been in the Soviet Union, having taken part in the Russian civil war and been responsible for mass reprisals against the White army and their supporters in Crimea (which Churchill would have been very aware of). At the time of writing the article, Churchill should have known that Kun had already fallen out of favour with many in the Soviet Communist Party and the exiled Hungarian communist movement for opposing the adoption of the Popular Front policy by the Comintern. Within a year of writing, both Trotsky and Kun were to be found guilty in Stalin's show trials. It seems as if Churchill had chosen the two of them to be his bogeymen because he had faced both when leading the British involvement in the Russian civil war in the early 1920s. Neither were particularly appropriate within the Spanish context. Churchill's inability to grasp any detail of left politics is also evident in his statement.

The British Government greeted the failed coup evolving

into a civil war in a similar way to Winston Churchill, that is giving an outward appearance of near neutrality but in reality, favouring the Nationalists over the Republicans, to a lesser or greater extent. As Prime Minister, Baldwin did not have a grasp of the detail of foreign affairs and lent heavily on others. The Foreign Secretary at the time, Anthony Eden first reported to the Cabinet on the coup on 22nd July, but the foreign office had been aware of it for some time. Harold Paterson, the British consul in Tenerife sent a telegram on the 18th and again on the 20th, following up with a detailed account a few days later. In this he refers to Bebb and his plane being "commandeered" by Franco, which was of course nonsense. In London, a foreign office diplomat wrote a note on the report which shows up the "commandeering" for the fabrication for what it was when he stated,

"It is interesting and strange that the Spanish Government's suspicions about Major Pollard's aeroplane date from the 16th July, 2 days before Gen Franco commandeered it. Possible there was some pre-arrangement."[11]

One piece of advice that Baldwin did give Eden was which side of the conflict Britain was not to be on. Baldwin stated on 26th July, "I told Eden yesterday that on no account, French or other, must he bring us into the fight on the side of the Russians."[12]

British Airways had been asked by Franco to sell four aircraft (non-military) to the Nationalists in order to help airlift the stranded soldiers of the Army of Africa to the Spanish mainland. This was raised by Eden at the Cabinet meeting of the 29th July. The British Government saw no reason to interfere in a civil, commercial transaction, effectively allowing British companies to actively assist in the overthrow of a democratic European

---

11 TNA: FO371/2025W7476
12 K. Middlemass and J. Barnes, *Baldwin, A Biography*, p 96.

Position No. 1: Churchill backs the Nationalists

government. The same Cabinet meeting also considered the legitimate right of the Spanish Government to buy military equipment from Britain. The Cabinet decided that in theory this would be permissible (in accordance with international law), however there was nothing that Britain had that was spare just now and so could not sell the Republic anything.

Any study of British foreign policy at the time of the coup would show that there was not much hope of Baldwin's Government backing the Republic. One of the reasons was the British attitude towards Italy. In December 1935, Britain had suffered the humiliation of newspapers revealing the secret Hoare-Laval Pact, which sought to bring an end Italy's war in Abyssinia by giving large parts of the African country over to Mussolini. The plan was appeasement in action, with devastating consequences for a smaller, independent nation. The British Cabinet with grave misgivings had decided to support the plan, in order to save the foreign minister's embarrassment at having the agreement he had negotiated rejected by his own country. However, it had leaked and the Government faced opposition from inside and outside the Conservative Party. It was also strongly criticised in France. The British were forced to withdraw the plan and Hoare resigned as Foreign Secretary in December 1935, to be succeeded by Anthony Eden. Italy renewed their attack on Abyssinia, using poisoned gas and eventually conquered the country in May 1936. Relations between Britain and Italy were greatly strained over the fiasco of the Hoare-Laval Pact. Britain's main foreign policy aim with regards to Italy was to stop the country allying with Germany and if possible, drive a wedge between Hitler and Mussolini. When it came to the conflict in Spain, the British government did not want to be involved, in any way which would alienate the Italians further. This was to cause tension within the British Cabinet as Italy's involvement in the Spanish Civil War grew.

This was also Churchill's position and one which he backed with speeches in the House of Commons against sanctions on Italy (imposed by the league of Nations when Italy initially invaded Abyssinia in October 1935) and against the strengthening of those sanctions by Britain by including oil. Although Britain outwardly supported the League and imposed sanctions against Italy, they did not include oil, which was most critical to Mussolini's military operation in Africa. This dismayed the opposition, but the Government were supported by Churchill. Nothing was to be done which might push Italy towards Germany, "We cannot have any anxieties comparable to the anxiety caused by German rearmament."[13]

One of the problems with this was that it was appeasement of a dictator, supported not just by the British Government as part of their policy but also by Churchill, who many regard as a (very near) lone voice against the policy in the mid-1930s. This view of Churchill does not align with the facts. Churchill was not against appeasement, he was against German military expansion and a ruthless dictator such as Mussolini could take over a small independent country by the most brutal means, using aerial bombardment and poisoned gas, just so long as Germany was not strengthened by it. One of the dilemmas for Churchill posed by Spain is that Italy and Germany were fighting on the same side from practically the very beginning and yet, initially at least, Churchill supported that side against the elected Government of the country.

In Spain, once the reality of the attempted coup had sunk in – and this was sooner for some than others – there was a response from the organised working class. The political parties, trade unions and other organisations set up militia and worked on defences for their area. In some places however they went much further. In Catalonia and Aragon in particular (but also

---

13 In Andrew Roberts, *Churchill*, p 393.

Position No. 1: Churchill backs the Nationalists

spread further than this), there was effectively a revolutionary takeover of civil society as well as a spontaneous mobilisation, indeed the two were inseparable in these areas. The Republican government was no longer in effective control in many places however this did not mean they descended into chaos. It could more accurately be argued that the revolutionary structures put in place to govern and take decisions helped to bring an end to the uncertainty and turmoil caused by the Generals' rising. This gave the people in these areas not only something to fight against (the common enemy of the Nationalists and the more general threat of fascism) but also something to fight for, to protect their revolution rather than merely on behalf of a bourgeois democracy, as they saw it. As Orwell put it when he arrived in Barcelona, "The working class were in the saddle."[14]

In many other places, even where the Republican government remained in control, there was collectivisation of farms and factories to a greater or lesser extent. The 'war or revolution' debate was a major dividing point among the Left in Spain throughout most of the first year of the war. Essentially, the anarchist and POUM position was that the upheaval caused by the Generals revolt has sparked a proletarian response which has rejected both the fascist coup and the bourgeois state. The best way to defeat the Nationalists, they argued, was to harness the power of the revolution which would not only ensure an equitable division of resources but provide motivation for those engaged in the deadly struggle against the fascist military forces. On the other side of the argument were the republicans (such as Azaña), the socialists (with some reluctance among more radical elements) and, most vociferously, the communists. Their argument was, put all our efforts into winning the war first and then we can decide what sort of society we want to build after that. The other reason for promoting this argument was that

---

14 George Orwell, *Homage to Catalonia.*

they needed to attract support from other countries. From an outside perspective, the Republican leadership were keen to portray Spain as part of the European family of democracies rather than a threat. It is one of the tragic ironies of Churchill's misjudged view that he was warning of a communist revolution when the communist party were suppressing it.

Franco had only been in Morocco for a day when he was given another piece of personal good fortune when the Head of the coup, General Sanjurjo, was killed on the 20th of July. Bebb had headed to Portugal from Morocco to collect the man who believed he would be the next Head of State and bring him to Spain. However General Mola had also sent the pilot, Juan Antonio Ansaldo to collect Sanjurjo in a small biplane. This seemed a more fitting and romantic way for Sanjurjo to enter Spain again and take over as leader of the country. The General therefore declined to travel with Bebb in the much larger Dragon Rapide. Sanjurjo preferred to return to Spain with a Spanish pilot who had greeted him as the leader of Spain rather than the Englishman Bebb; stepping out of the small biplane seemed more heroic and fitting for his triumphant return to the country than arriving in a modern British plane with an English pilot. Fatally, Sanjurjo, who was an extremely heavy man, insisted on taking his dress uniforms, which also weighed a lot. He said that he wanted to the look the part as the new caudillo of Spain. (There is no precise equivalent of caudillo in English, it means a strong military leader, like a warlord). The weight of Sanjurjo and his luggage proved too much for the small biplane and it crashed on take-off from Estoril. Although sabotage has been suspected, there is no evidence of this. Sanjurjo had been killed by his own vanity in both his choice of plane and his choice of regalia. The figurehead of the coup and would-be Head of State was dead; the political darling of the Right, Calvo Sotelo had of course been killed just before the coup. The Generals tasked with

Position No. 1: Churchill backs the Nationalists

taking Spain's two largest cities, Goded in Madrid and Fanjul in Barcelona – both senior to Franco – failed in their objective and by the middle of August both had been killed. This only left two possible rivals for Franco in his bid to become caudillo, if the Nationalists won the war: General Mola and the Falange leader, Jose Antonio Primo de Rivera. Within a year both of them were dead.

8
FAMILY TIES

There were a number of people involved in the Spanish Civil War who could claim some type of kinship with either Churchill or Franco. Five of them are discussed below: Ramón and Nicolás Franco, brothers of Francisco; Esmond Romilly, Churchill's nephew; Serrano Suñer, Franco's brother-in-law; and the Duke of Alba, Franco's representative in Britain - a man that Churchill called cousin. It is worth briefly first mentioning one other person with a family connection, for his participation in the conflict was indeed short.

Franco's first cousin, Major Ricardo de la Puente Bahamonde was in many ways more like a brother to Franco than cousin. Growing up, they had often been together, and Ricardo was described as Franco's closest childhood friend. Both were in the military, but Franco knew that Ricardo's politics were a little more progressive than his own. When given the responsibility of suppressing the miners involved in the Asturias revolt in 1934, Franco suspected that his cousin, at that time in charge of the air force in León, would not order his pilots to fire on civilians and so had him replaced. Franco had no such qualms and shelled working class districts. By July 1936, de la Puente was stationed in Morocco. At the beginning of the rising, he had held the airport at Tetuán for the Republic. When he realised that the airport was going to fall into the hands of the Nationalists, he sabotaged the planes so as to deny them to the forces of the attempted coup. For this brave act, and for remaining loyal to the Republic, Ricardo de la Puente was arrested by the rebels who took the airport. When Franco arrived, de la Puente was undergoing a summary court martial. The verdict was that he was to be shot. Franco, as commander had the power to veto this but chose not to. A few years earlier, during one of their disagreements as adults over politics, Franco had apparently said to his cousin, "one day, I am going to have you shot." Ricardo's sentence was carried out at the beginning of August 1936.

The Brothers

Ramón Franco (see Chapter 2) had been a national hero, eclipsing older brother Francisco, for his exploits as a pilot. In the mid-1920s, few events around the world caught the imagination of the public as much as the daring exploits of pilots who pushed the boundaries of air travel. In 1926, a year before Charles Lindberg's transatlantic flight in the Spirit of St. Louis made him a global superstar, Ramón was the pilot for a daring journey by air from Spain to Argentina. Along with the rest of the crew, Ramón became the first to fly the route between the two countries, successfully bridging the gap between the old world and the new in under 60 hours. Stopping off in the Canary islands, Cape Verde, Rio de Janeiro and Montevideo, they were making aviation history and breaking records. They instantly became huge celebrities and were adored in Spain and Argentina in particular. Such was Ramón's fame that even when Francisco was leading the army of Africa for the Nationalists at the beginning of the Spanish Civil War ten years later, the Times in London referred to General Franco as the famous aviator's brother.

Ramón had fallen from grace in his own country when he took part in attempts to overthrow, or at least undermine the monarchy, in 1930 and had to flee Spain. He returned after the Republic was declared and was readmitted to the military but dismissed following his part in an anarchist plot. Ramón was a Deputy in the Cortes for the Republican Left of Catalonia. When the attempted coup began, Ramón was an air attaché for Spain in the United States. When he returned, he eschewed his left-wing politics when he joined his brother's side. This familial loyalty was reciprocated when Franco put him in charge of the airbase in Mallorca and promoted him to Lieutenant Colonel. This enraged many of the other Nationalist airmen, as Ramón was a disgraced, former officer who was also a freemason and former left-wing Republican. Ramón died when his plane crashed off the coast of Mallorca in October 1938.

Nicolás was the eldest of the five children (the brothers also had two sisters) and his father's favourite, for whom he was named. He became a naval engineer and took after his father in personality, being carefree with money and a womaniser. At the start of the Civil War, Nicolás was a keen supporter of his brother and happy to take a subservient role to his younger sibling. He became part of a small group surrounding Franco who pushed him forward, firstly as the head of the Nationalist army and then as Head of State. In the crucial meeting of the leaders of the Nationalists in September 1936, from which Franco emerged as Generalisimo, the highest of the Generals, it was Nicolás who returned from Portugal, having met there with the German and Italian ambassadors, to declare that Germany and Italy wanted a single, unified command and they wanted that leader to be Franco. As the machinations continued, the others (some reluctantly) agreed that Franco would not only be the commander of the armed forces, but also the Head of the Government of the Spanish State. Franco had gone from reluctant conspirator to undisputed leader of the Nationalists and effectively Head of State in waiting, in just a few months.

Nicolás made the first tentative steps to secure a political base for Franco soon afterwards. However, setting up a right of centre party, inevitably similar to the previous CEDA group, would have brought the hostility of the Falange, who were growing in both number and importance. It was not until

Serrano Suñer became part of the inner circle (see below) that moves could properly be made to enable this. Nicolás continued to make himself useful to Franco throughout the civil war and while he lacked the sophisticated talents of Serrano Suñer, he was completely trusted and remained one of the tight inner circle. Nicolás played a major part in the treachery involving the taking of the Basque country by the Nationalists. He had promised the Basque leaders that if they surrendered, there would be no reprisals and political opponents of the Nationalists could leave as refugees. Nicolás repeated this to the Italians who, in due course, accepted the Basque surrender. They were horrified when Franco forced the fleeing opponents off of British ships they had embarked on and tried them, executing many. Franco pretended to know nothing of Nicolás's promise, though it has clearly been part of an agreed strategy.

Franco wanted to give his brother a key position when he formed his first proper Cabinet, but Serrano Suñer persuaded him not to, on the grounds of not wanting to appear too nepotistic. Franco made Nicolás his ambassador to Portugal instead. Nicolás helped to negotiate the Iberian Pact of March 1939, which cemented relationships between Franco's Spain and Portugal, which had supported the Nationalists throughout the Civil War.

The Nephew

Esmond Romilly was Churchill's nephew on his wife, Clementine's side, though the relationship between the two men was closer than that suggests. Growing up, Esmond spent a number of holidays and family occasions at Chartwell, the Churchill's country home, with his cousins and aunt and uncle. As he grew, there was a resemblance between Esmond and Winston and rumours spread that Churchill was actually the boy's father. It is certainly true that Clementine's sister, Nellie, Esmond's mother, had numerous affairs and it is doubtful if any of the four children she had were fathered by her husband, Colonel Bertrand Romilly. Nellie published a thinly disguised biographical novel which said as much. However, apart from the physical similarities and the opportunity afforded by familial proximity, there is no hard evidence to support the claim about Winston being Emond's father. It is true that Nellie adored Winston and often compared him favourably to her own husband however, Romilly's biographer and Churchill's principal ones dispute it. What is clear is that Esmond worshipped his uncle, regardless of political differences. There cannot have been many schoolboys who had a photograph of Winston Churchill and a bust of Lenin beside their beds, as Esmond did at Wellington school.

As an 18-year-old, in October 1936, Esmond left his job at *World Film News* and headed to join the fight in Spain. After some training at the International Brigades camp at Albacete, Romilly moved with his companions to the battle of Madrid in the early part of November. His first action was in defence of Nationalist attempts to take the Madrid to Valencia road. The Republican Government, fearing that Madrid was going to be captured, had moved to Valencia making this road a strategic means of supply and communication between the Government and the traditional Spanish capital. From that first taste of war, Esmond moved with his company to Madrid itself where he took part in the fierce, chaotic fighting in the University City area. The Nationalist advance was halted, with the International Brigades playing an important role, alongside militias and loyal troops, saving Madrid for the Republic.

Romilly took part in other engagements and in mid-December 1936, along with the rest of the British section of the German Thälmann Battalion as part of the XIIth Brigade (the British Battalion was not officially formed until early 1937, as part of the XVth Brigade, see Chapter 13) Romilly fought at

Boadilla del Monte to the West of Madrid. Attempting to stop a rebel advance, the British came under heavy fire and most were killed, including Romilly's close friend, Joe. Mentally and physically exhausted after several days of battle, Romilly was taken back to Albacete and then to hospital in Madrid, suffering from dysentery. He returned to Britain to recuperate in January 1937 but was determined to return to Spain, this time as a war correspondent. It was while convalescing at his cousin Dorothy's house that he met and fell in love with someone who would not only change his life but bring him into the public eye even more than before.

Jessica (known as Decca) Mitford was one of the famous Mitford sisters, rarely far from the society pages. Two of her sisters were supporters of fascism, with one, Diana, having married British fascist leader, Oswald Moseley the year before. Decca however was a communist and had admired Esmond (they were second cousins) from afar for some time. They eloped to France, *en route* to Spain. Although they arrived in the Basque country, their stay in Spain was short-lived as the press had picked up the story and were reporting the scandal of a peer's daughter running off to the war in Spain with Winston Churchill's nephew. A destroyer was sent to pick the couple up and they reluctantly agreed to leave on it to save their Basque hosts from any embarrassment. Returned to France, both families tried to persuade the couple to give up their relationship but eventually realised their protestations were futile and, with Decca pregnant, both the mother of the bride and the mother of the groom were present in France when Esmond and Jessica married in May 1937. Esmond did not return to Spain. Following the death of their infant daughter later that year of measles, the couple moved to America. During the second World War, Esmond joined the Canadian air force and took part in several missions over occupied Europe and Germany. It was during one such flight, on 30th November 1941, Winston Churchill's 67th birthday, that Esmond's plane was lost over the North Sea with no survivors.

The Brother-in-law

One of the architects of the Franco regime which followed the civil war and a major player in Franco's camp during it, was his brother-in-law, Ramón Serrano Suñer. Franco had first met Serrano Suñer in Zaragoza in 1931 when the latter was a lawyer and Franco was the Director of the Military Academy. Serrano Suñer became a frequent guest in the Franco household and there met Franco's wife's younger sister, Ramóna (known as Zita). The couple were married in February 1932. The witnesses were Franco (for the bride) and Jose Antonio Primo de Rivera for the groom (Serrano Suñer and Jose Antonio had studied together in Madrid). The wedding was the first time Franco had met the son of the recent dictator, future founding leader of the Falange.

Serrano Suñer became a Depute in the Cortes, supporting CEDA after the 1933 election and then as a supporter of the Falange (though not standing for election as such) in 1936. He was instrumental in persuading most of the youth wing of CEDA, the JAP, to move *en masse* over to the Falange in the Spring of 1936, following CEDA's defeat by the Popular Front. At the outbreak of the civil war, Serrano Suñer and his family were in the Republican zone and he was arrested and imprisoned, along with his brothers. Two of his brothers were killed, being taken out of prison and shot, as happened to a number of prisoners in Republican jails in the early days of the civil war, as reprisals for atrocities by Nationalist troops. Fearing the same might happen to him, Serrano Suñer played down any links between himself and his brother-in-law. In fact, Serrano Suñer had acted as a go-between, passing messages from Franco to Mola and back again during the plotting of the coup. He was not told the date of the coup however and could not save himself and his family.

Serrano Suñer managed to escape from prison and make his way to Salamanca, where Franco had his headquarters, in February 1937.

Serrano Suñer then became, "the brains behind the creation of a new political movement, and, indeed, chief architect of the Francoist state."[1] He decided to wholeheartedly work for not only the Nationalist cause, but Franco. For his part, Franco knew that his brother-in-law was much more intellectually capable than he was himself but did not feel threatened by him, because Serrano Suñer had no independent power base of his own. Franco also recognised that Serrano Suñer's friendship with Jose Antonio de Rivera could help cement a link between Franco and the Falange. Until his brother-in-law's arrival, Franco had concentrated on consolidating military leadership and power, now he could look at building a State structure. Serrano Suñer had meetings with Mola, the Carlists, monarchists, the Church and the Falange. He began to set out – and help bring about – a new administration which would be capable of seamlessly transitioning from war into a post-war period. In assuming this role, he was to an extent usurping Franco's brother Nicolás, who until then had been responsible for leading the administration under Franco. Nicolás was not capable of creating a whole new State structure and was also wary of putting anything in place which might undermine Franco's position. Until then, Franco was head of the Nationalist side in the Civil War, chosen by a small group of Generals, largely because of the expediency of the continuing flow of German and Italian aid through Franco. There was little open discussion and fewer plans for what came next. Serrano Suñer changed all this and not only "invented" the Spain that would emerge from the Civil War, but helped ensure that Franco would be the undisputed head of it. Franco became the Caudillo of Spain, with Suñer nicknamed the *Cuñadisimo*

---

[1] Paul Preston, *Franco*, p 253.

(highest brother-in-law) as a play on Franco's title of *Generalisimo*. Suñer was eventually sacrificed by Franco, as the Dictator tried to back-pedal frantically from supporting the Axis powers during World War II, once he realised that the Allies might win the war (See Chapter 16). Suñer's links to Germany and Italy made him a convenient scapegoat and he resigned as foreign minister and President of the political council of the Falange in September 1942, after a grenade was thrown by a Falangist in an attempt to kill a Carlist officer and his supporters. Franco later tried to play down his own links to Hitler and Mussolini, blaming much of it on Suñer.

The "Cousin"

The Duke of Alba, (the 17th of that title, he was also the 10th Duke of Berwick) was a Spanish nobleman of the first rank. Educated in England, he was an anglophile who served firstly as Franco's representative in Britain and then as Spain's ambassador to Britain during the second World War. Named Jacobo Fitz-James Stuart y Falcó, he was a Jacobite and direct descendent of James VII of Scotland (James II of England) through (as his name suggests) an illegitimate offspring, in this case a child James fathered with Arabella Churchill, the sister of the first Duke of Marlborough. Winston Churchill was the grandson of the 7th Duke of Marlborough and referred to the Duke of Alba as 'cousin', when he wasn't calling him 'Jimmy'. Bound by class, family and monarchist inclination (the Duke had served as foreign minister under Alfonso until shortly before the King stepped down in 1931), Churchill and the Duke got on well, although the Duke of Alba moved very comfortably among all of the British ruling class. Many considered him the true King of Scotland, although he never pressed the title himself.

It was this ease of access to the British establishment that put Franco at a distinct advantage over the Republicans when it came to courting favour in Britain. Long before the Civil War, the Duke was briefing against the Republic and once war broke out, a quiet conversation in the dining room of a London Gentlemen's club in favour of the Nationalists was worth far more than noisy protests in the street about aiding the Republic. The Duke found a reception for his version of events, with Chamberlain and especially Lord Halifax (who replaced Eden as foreign secretary in February 1938) but in truth almost all of the Conservatives were more inclined to listen to a Royal Duke than a representative of a workers' government. It was much the same bonds that meant that Lord Halifax was also perfectly comfortable taking a hunting trip with Hermann Goring in November 1937. The British ambassador in Spain happily agreed to take the Duke of Alba's art collection into the British Embassy for safe keeping, in case it fell into the hands of the reds. Churchill wrote that "naturally, I was not in favour of the Communists (sic). How could I be, when if I had been a Spaniard they would have murdered me and my family and friends?"[2] Leaving aside whether that is true or not (Churchill had the death of the Duke of Alba's younger brother to support his argument) it shows the perspective from which Churchill viewed the Spanish conflict. It was class war in his eyes, and he knew which class he belonged to.

---

2 Winston Churchill, *The Gathering Storm*, p 192.

9
POSITION NO. 2: NON-INTERVENTION

Following Churchill's initial thoughts on the outbreak of the conflict (see chapter 7) he wrote several times more on the Spanish Civil war throughout 1936. Less than a fortnight after "The Spanish Tragedy", Churchill wrote a piece called, "Keep out of Spain" on the 21st August. In this, Churchill gave his wholehearted support to non-intervention in the Spanish conflict, though his reasoning was as flawed and as twisted as in his previous piece. Again, his purpose was to try to persuade people against the natural sympathy that most had for Republican Spain. An embattled democracy facing not just its own traitorous Generals and their followers but increasingly the forces of the German and Italian dictators. There are several points that Churchill gets wrong and most of them are uncorrected in The Gathering Storm written after the war. Firstly, Churchill thought that the war was "rolling steadily towards its climax"[1] though he said that the struggle may be prolonged. Churchill also states that "it seems certain that a majority of Spaniards are on the rebel side."[2]

To try to support this assertion, Churchill quotes figures for the election stating that four and a half million voted for the "Right and Centre" against four and a quarter million for the parties of the Left. Leaving aside his figures (which were incorrect), there were two assumptions that Churchill was making which were clearly unsupportable. The first is that all

---
1 Winston Churchill, *Step by Step*, p 42.
2 *Ibid.* p 42.

those who voted for the Right would support the Nationalists. The Falange vote in the 1936 election was miniscule (less than a half of one percent). They were the only party on the Right advocating a violent overthrow of the Government. The largest party on the Right were CEDA. It is certainly true that the leader, Gil Robles, was an admirer of Hitler and believed that the best way for the Right to gain power was to become the government and then change the rules so that they could not be removed (as Hitler had done). Robles supported the conspiracy and the coup however it is much less certain that all of CEDA's conservative Catholic voters would have done. It is a big step from wanting the continuation of traditional social norms to violently overthrowing the Government. The Republic had been declared among huge popular support (despite what Churchill had stated in *Great Contemporaries*) and there was overwhelming support for its continuation. This had been shown at the reaction to the Sanjurjada, when an outpouring of relief for the saving of the Republic had accompanied the defeat of the General Sanjurjo's attempted coup in 1932. Although there had been a polarisation by 1936, there is no evidence that most of the ordinary voters on the Right supported a violent overthrow of the Government, as can be seen by the refusal of the outgoing administration to countenance the use of troops to maintain them in power after the February elections.

Churchill's second assumption was that the Centre parties and their voters would have supported the coup. This is an even more fanciful notion. The Centre parties were all committed to democracy and were supporters of the Republic as an ideal. There was no backing among them for any kind of extra-parliamentary activity to thwart the will of the people in the election. Most of them had entered the election in 1936 on a platform that specifically rejected uprisings of the left or right and were determined to use democracy to prevent them. The

Position No. 2: Non-Intervention

Party of the Democratic Centre (the largest Centre Party) and the Progressive Republicans were against the coup. Even the Catholic Basque Nationalist Party supported the Republic and fought against the Nationalists in the Civil War.

What is interesting in this piece by Churchill is his acknowledgement that the Nationalists were being supplied by Germany and Italy.

"They (the Nationalists) have no doubt received important supplies of munitions and aeroplanes from German and Italian sources."[3]

German and Italian aid had been essential in the first mass airlift of troops in history, when Franco's Army of Africa transported across the Straits of Gibraltar. Franco made several attempts to obtain aircraft from Italy in those early days. Through Italian contacts in North Africa and via Bolin who arrived in Rome carrying Franco's scribbled plea for assistance, he was initially rebuffed several times by Mussolini. Il Duce had been led up the garden path too many times by Spanish Rightists claiming that they were on the verge of revolution if only he would support them. Bolin tried to convince the Italian foreign minister, Ciano, and Mussolini that with Sanjurjo gone, Franco would be the leader of the coup. Meanwhile General Mola, unaware of Franco's efforts, had sent a delegation of monarchists to see the Italians (and to Berlin to meet with the German leaders) to plead for aid for the Nationalist cause. Mola's request was of a smaller scale (for bullets rather than bombers) and with France apparently poised to aid the Republic, Mussolini finally agreed to send 12 aircraft to Franco on the 28th of July. Three of the aircraft ran out of fuel on the way there and the others had to wait for a tanker of fuel to arrive from Sardinia, however they were soon joined by German aircraft. A direct appeal from Franco via a delegation flown to Germany who

---

3 Winston Churchill, *Step by Step*, p 43.

managed to meet with Hitler saw him commit to the Nationalist cause on 25th July and send 20 transport planes rather than the ten requested. Operation Magic Fire began, which would see the Germans essentially save the stalled coup by swiftly bringing the Army of Africa to the Spanish mainland over the next few weeks. Those not transported in the German Junkers Ju-52/3m planes, sailed over under the cover of the Italian bombers and the close proximity of German warships.

The crucial factors in both Germany and Italy in backing Franco specifically rather than Mola was the boldness of his approach and the fact that he headed the best part of the Spanish fighting forces. In 1942, Hitler told Franco that he should "erect a monument to the glory of the Junkers Ju-52. It is this aircraft that the Spanish revolution has to thank for its victory".[4] While the aid was crucial at this early stage, it would prove to be overwhelming in the long run. What was equally important, from Franco's point of view, is that the aid came through him. This was the main reason that he became the undisputed leader of the Nationalists in the war, and which laid the foundation for him to move from being the Generalissimo to being the Caudillo later.

Churchill tried to create a false equivalence which was just not true in August 1936, referring to help from Soviet Russia for the Republic. The first shipment of supplies from the Soviet Union did not arrive in Spain until October. Much of the thrust of Churchill's article however was aimed at France. At the start of the rising by the Generals, France had rushed to give aid to its fellow Popular Front Government to the South. On the 19th of July, Giral had sent a telegram to Blum (the French Premier) requesting 20 bombers, field guns, machine guns, rifles and ammunition. Blum arranged to send this with his aviation minister in secret because of the volatile political situation in

---

4 *Hitler's Table Talk*, p 687.

Position No. 2: Non-Intervention

France at the time, with the fascist Croix de Feu and others, and counter violence by Communist groups. This was not to be the first of many transfers of war materiel. Under increasing pressure from right-wing newspapers and others, Blum agreed to only allow private sales of unarmed aeroplanes. This was intolerable to the Spanish Republicans as it put them on the same footing as the Nationalists.

The pressure on the French Government was not all internal. Britain worked very hard to ensure that France was not "dragged in" to the Spanish conflict and made certain that they knew that Britain would not come to their aid if they were fighting a proxy war with the dictators through Spain. The British foreign secretary, Anthony Eden, persuaded the French that left to their own devices, neither side could win in Spain and therefore the best way that France could help would be to ensure that no country sent armaments to either side. On 25th July, the French accepted that they would no longer supply the Spanish Republic. In putting forward this notion, Eden may well have been correct and some sort of negotiated settlement would have been the result of the current stalemate, however it ignored two crucial factors. Firstly, the legitimate Spanish Government had a right in international law, to purchase armaments to supress a coup from among its own armed forces. Secondly, the Germans and Italians were supplying aid to the Nationalists. This had been proven from the start when one of the initial group of 12 Italian planes had been forced to crash land in French Morocco and one of the first of the German planes had been blown off course into Republican held Spain.

On 2nd August, a policy of non-intervention was proposed by the French. The idea was that France, Britain, Germany and Italy were to agree not to supply arms to either side in the Spanish conflict. Part of the French thinking was that German military supplies would be superior to those of France and they would therefore be aiding the Spanish Republic if they kept everyone out of the war. It was of course a forlorn hope. Over the next few days, the French sounded out the Germans and Italians on the idea. Both of the dictatorships stalled on a definite reply while they intensified their arms supplies to the Nationalists. No such surge was forthcoming for the Republic. The British put further pressure on the French who banned even the sale of commercial aircraft to the Republic (although Britain had allowed this for the Nationalists from British companies only days before). On 8th August, the French closed the Spanish border to all prohibited goods. Four days later, the French proposed setting up an international committee to oversee the upholding of any non-intervention agreement. Eden unilaterally banned the supply of any armaments to the Republic and refused to admit that there was any evidence of Germany and Italy supplying the Nationalists. Baldwin apparently told the French ambassador that he would prefer a rebel victory to a Republican one; and he certainly warned the Labour opposition that any statement of sympathy for the Republic would be against British interests and therefore unpatriotic.

Before the end of August, all of the major countries, including Britain, France, Germany, Italy and the Soviet Union, along with several other countries, had agreed to non-intervention. It seems clear though that the Germans and Italians only signed once they were sure that there would be few consequences for breaches of the agreement by them. Germany had told the British that they had not supplied anything to the Nationalists and never would. They said that the plane that had been captured by the Republic had been a commercial transport plane and demanded its return before signing. Thus, the policy of non-intervention was born. Part of the overall policy of appeasement of the dictators and signalling the slow death of the Spanish Republic.

Position No. 2: Non-Intervention

It was non-intervention that Winston Churchill was referring to in his "Keep out of Spain" article. Written as the details of the policy were being formalised, Churchill expressed some sympathy with the French Premier but even at this stage, he could see the policy was unlikely to work:
"Great allowances must be made for the difficulties of M. Blum. It is earnestly hoped that even if Germany and Italy on the one hand, and Soviet Russia on the other, send help to their respective factions and fence disingenuously with proposals for a collective neutrality, France will none the less adopt the same attitude of detachment as Great Britain. A serious divergence between the two powerful Parliamentary countries of the Western World would be the last disaster... there is only one rule for the Liberal Parliamentary countries: Send charitable aid under the Red Cross to both sides, and for the rest, Keep out of it and arm."[5]

This was an espousal of the policy of appeasement, later criticised by Churchill but here laid out clearly. Regardless of the military actions of Hitler and Mussolini, even on the continent of Europe, Great Britain and France should not intervene but instead should arm against a future conflict. This despite the German and Italian interventions making their own armed forces better prepared and more battle ready. It is precisely the policy continued by Chamberlain when he became Prime Minister in May 1937 and for which he was blamed as one of the 'guilty men' who had allowed the growth of Nazi Germany and the coming of the second World War.

Churchill wrote several more times regarding Spain before the year was out. In a piece from 18th September entitled, "A testing time for France", Churchill compared Spain and her people very unfavourably to France.

"The whole character of French society is incomparably superior to that of Spain in moral quality, in military power, in

---

5 Winston Churchill *Keep out of Spain* in *Step by Step*, p 45.

urbanity, experience and intelligence."⁶

He returned to the subject of Spain again at the beginning of October, at a time when the Republic seemed doomed. In this, Churchill tried to shift blame for the Generals' revolt on to the Republican Government, ignoring the plotting that had been happening for months and believing that:

"The whole army obeyed the orders of their generals... every garrison mutinied dutifully."⁷

This is Churchill rewriting history. More Generals had stayed loyal to the Republic than had actually supported the coup. The army on the mainland had been split, with only the Army of Africa giving the Nationalists the numerical advantage. Churchill went on to berate the atrocities committed on the Republican side, virtually ignoring those by the Nationalists. He completely mischaracterised Largo Caballero, who had taken over as Prime Minister of the Spanish Republic and Minister of War on the 4th of September. Churchill said that Largo Caballero:

"Is now engaged in the double task of carrying forward the Marxian revolution and defending the contracting circular front around Madrid."⁸

Churchill was not alone in believing that Madrid could soon be encircled and captured, he was however incorrect about the priority of the new Spanish Premier. Largo Caballero was not a Communist and in the 'war or revolution' debate he wanted to win the war first (as the Communists themselves did) In October, he created the new Republican People's army, merging the loyal remnants of the previous Spanish army (which had been dissolved in July) with the militias. This brought a much more organised approach to the defence of the Republic and slowed the seemingly unstoppable advance of the Nationalists.

---

6 Winston Churchill in *A testing Time for France* in *Step by Step*, p 52.
7 Winston Churchill in *An Object Lesson from Spain* in *Step by Step*, p 54.
8 Winston Churchill in *An Object Lesson from Spain* in *Step by Step*, p 55.

Position No. 2: Non-Intervention

Churchill commented in the article on Franco's ambiguous letter to the Republican Government sent a few weeks before the coup in which he warned that some people were plotting and that he could be trusted to put this down if called upon. Churchill missed the point of this however, believing that this was sent on behalf of the plotters when this was Franco's own scheme and typical of his duplicitous behaviour. Franco had still been hedging his bets then and as we know did not finally decide to join the coup until a few days before. The thrust of Churchill's argument in this piece however is the barbarity of the atrocities committed in the Republican zone and how these were worse than anything done by the Nationalists.

"Although it seems to be the practice of the Nationalists to shoot a proportion of their prisoners taken in arms, they cannot be accused of having fallen to the level of committing the atrocities which are the daily handiwork of the Communists, Anarchists and the POUM… It would be a mistake alike in truth and wisdom for British public opinion to rate both sides at the same level."

With hindsight we know that there were killings of unarmed people on both sides however there was a difference and not just in numbers, with the Nationalists killing far more. The terror that the Nationalists caused by their murder of civilians in captured areas was a deliberate policy of the leadership rather than the spontaneous work of militias, as many of those in the Republican zone were. The Nationalists wanted the civilian population to flee before them, giving the Republicans more and more mouths to feed in a decreasing area. To do this, they used mass killings, rape and torture as deliberate weapons of war, not only sanctioned but ordered by their leaders. Franco stated in July that he would happily shoot half of Spain to achieve victory. Churchill was correct that the British public should not rate both sides at the same level, but not in the way he intended. In their defence, Churchill and the British Government were receiving very biased reports from the British Ambassador (who moved to base himself in Hendaye, France rather than stay in Madrid when it was controlled by the Republic) and the Naval commanders in Gibraltar, all firm supporters of the Nationalists. However, much of the barbarity of the Nationalists would have been known to Churchill at this time and he has allowed his instinctive class and political prejudices to tarnish his writing. He regularly met with Franco's representatives in Britain (including Churchill's 'cousin' the Duke of Alba) while he refused to even shake hands with the official ambassador of the Spanish Republican Government to Britain in the autumn of 1936.

10
ITALY AT WAR WITH THE SPANISH REPUBLIC AND THE FLIGHT OF THE CONDOR

As we have seen, from a very early point, Mussolini decided to back the Nationalists and to do so only through Franco. The Italian dictator's motives were clear. He wanted Italy to become the dominant power in the Mediterranean with a navy to rival that of Britain and the ability to begin to harass the French in North Africa. The establishment of another fascist state in Iberia - one indebted to Mussolini – would be perfect to evict the British from Gibraltar and give him a naval base in the Balearics. Mussolini also had another reason for supporting the Nationalists. Italian and German relations had been strained over Austria and the British had sought to exploit this by trying to drive a wedge between the two dictators. Mussolini however was much more interested in currying favour with Hitler and thought that his best chance was to make Italy appear as a strong ally rather than another weak country that Hitler could dominate. Therefore, it was also to impress the Germans with their military prowess that Mussolini poured so much aid into Spain in support of the Nationalists. Best of all for Franco, most of the aid was virtually free. The initial consignment of 12 Italian planes was followed soon afterwards with over 30 fighter planes and some tanks and field guns. Italian aid continued, despite denials from their delegates at meetings of the non-intervention committee in London and was dramatically increased following two events.

The first was a secret agreement between Franco and Mussolini made at the end of November 1936. At this point in the war, events were not going well for Franco. He had failed, partly due to his personal choices and tactics, to take Madrid. The timely arrival of the first Soviet aid and the formation of the first of the International Brigades, alongside militias and regular army troops, helped the Republic to defend the city. Privately, some of Franco's generals believed that if the Republic had been able to counterattack at that point, the Nationalists would not have been able to hold them. Despite receiving large quantities of Italian and German aid, Franco was now desperate for more, but they were to come at a price. Until now, the Italian pilots and ground crew along with the army personnel who were there, had enlisted in the Spanish foreign legion and wore their uniforms. This helped the Italians keep up the pretence that they were not supplying the Nationalists, even though there was clear evidence that they were. Now however, Mussolini was to drop that particular charade, secure as he was in the knowledge that Britain was not going to do anything about breeches of the Non-Intervention agreement.

Mussolini insisted that there would be a separate Italian column led by Italian generals. He also wanted acknowledgement that Italy had supremacy in the Mediterranean. At this point a desperate Franco would have agreed to almost anything in order to obtain the supplies he needed to prevent the Nationalist advance being totally halted. Mussolini went from almost deciding to pull out of Spain to committing to the Nationalist cause even more, albeit with caveats.

The second event that made Mussolini commit even harder to achieving victory in Spain by greatly increasing Italian involvement, was, ironically, the victory of the Republicans at the battle of Guadalajara. The failure of the Nationalists to take

Madrid in 1936 led to them attempting to encircle it by cutting the Madrid to Valencia road. This resulted in a number of battles in early 1937, including the Battle of Jarama in February when the Nationalist advance was held off at the price of a large number of casualties, especially among the International Brigades. Heavy losses for both the British Battalion and the American Lincoln Battalion were inflicted, but the Nationalists failed to take their objective (See Chapter 13). Only a few weeks later, the Nationalists attempted to break the Republican lines some miles away at Guadalajara and suffered one of their worst defeats of the war. A mixture of poor tactics and poor weather meant that the Italian Nationalist troops, some of whom were in their tropical uniforms, believing they were going to Africa instead of Spain, were routed. In one of the great ironies of the Civil War, the Nationalist Italian troops of the Italian CTV were defeated by, in part at least, their fellow Italians in the Garibaldi Battalion of the XII International Brigade (See Chapter 13).

The CTV (*Corpo Truppe Voluntarie*) was the name given to the Italian forces that Mussolini sent following his secret agreement with Franco. The first 3000 of them landed in Spain in December 1936 and when renamed the CTV in February 1937, there were over 40 000 Italian troops fighting for the Nationalists and by the time of the Battle of Guadalajara, there were more than 50 000. Although there were some Italian fascist blackshirts who volunteered, the soldiers were mainly poor conscripts and there was nothing voluntary about their participation. The new Italian force had an early success in the beginning of February 1937 when alongside Nationalist troops from the Army of Africa, they captured the city and province of Malaga from the Republicans. The fall of Malaga was a disaster for the defending Republicans who had no match for the armoured assault of the Italians. The slaughter of those captured and the shelling, aerial and naval bombardment of the civilians who fled along the coast was horrific with several thousand killed.

The ease of victory in Malaga gave the Italians a false confidence ahead of the assault at Guadalajara. In early March, 35 000 Italian soldiers were available to commander, General Roatta, for the assault near Guadalajara, with 15 000 Nationalist Spanish troops in reserve, with a great many Italian armoured vehicles including light tanks and support from the Italian air force. The defending Republicans had around 10 000 men, a smaller number of armoured vehicles and a number of planes, mainly supplied by the Soviet Union. Another 10 000 were called upon to bolster the Republican defence. The initial attack on 8th of March saw a short but heavy artillery and aerial bombardment of Republican positions followed by an armoured advance which broke through Republican lines. Their advance was halted by fog and sleet.

The following day saw another Italian attack come to a stop as bad weather and poor visibility hampered the tanks. On 10th March, the Republicans were reinforced by Italians and Poles in the International Brigades, joining the French and Germans already fighting there. The Italians in the Garibaldi battalion were close enough to shout over to their countrymen to come and join them (See Chapter 13 for a full description of the International Brigades in this battle). On the 12th of March, a counterattack by the Republicans was successful as they had almost 100 Soviet planes, flown from the concrete airfield at Albacete, while the Italian planes were literally bogged down in their muddy airstrips. Over the next week or so, the Republicans advanced and the Italians, now supported by the reserve Spanish Nationalist troops, retreated, at times in panic. A force of around 20 000 Republican troops, many of them from the International Brigades, had defeated a mainly Italian Nationalist force of over twice as many. Former British Prime Minister, David Lloyd George, called it, "The Italian skedaddle".

Italy at War with the Spanish Republic

Coming so soon after Jarama, which although not an outright victory for the Republic had stopped the Nationalist advance, Guadalajara was another great morale boost and gave many hope that the Republic was not necessarily doomed. Franco was apparently ambiguous about the loss. He did not want Madrid taken by Italians and was worried about the perception, at home and abroad, that he could only win when using foreign forces. In some Nationalist Generals' quarters there were reports of toasts to the heroism of Spanish soldiers "of whatever colour", indicating their lack of enthusiasm for the Italians regardless of how much they needed them. There was certainly criticism of Franco among the Italian commanders for not launching an accompanying attack on the Jarama front, which allowed the Republic to move troops from there to reinforce those at Guadalajara.

In the longer term however, the Italian defeat at Guadalajara was an embarrassment that Mussolini was determined to erase. Having already committed an enormous quantity of men and machinery, Mussolini stated that not one Italian soldier would be allowed to leave Spain until victory over the Republic had erased the shame of Guadalajara. Paul Preston summed up the Italian commitment to the Nationalist cause thus: "By 1937, Italy was effectively at war with the Spanish Republic."[1]

At the beginning of the conflict, the Germans had been going through a very similar process to the Italians regarding aiding the Nationalists, at almost the exact same time. While General Mola's unambitious requests in July 1936 had never got further than being bogged down in low level bureaucracy, Franco's bolder steps were given the go ahead at the highest level. Hitler's motivation for supporting the Nationalists was initially anti-Bolshevism, the same instinct which put Churchill on that

---

1 Paul Preston, The Spanish Civil War: Reaction, Revolution and Revenge, p 158.

side too. German strategy in Spain was to develop however and there were a number of reasons for Hitler's support of Franco which went beyond the most obvious. In highlighting and exaggerating the threat in Spain from the Left, Hitler was able to play on the fears of British Conservatism and create a gap between British and French foreign policy. The opportunity to isolate France from Britain was a great prize for the Nazis, that the French were only too well aware of. France could not afford to lose Britain as her ally in an increasing dangerous Europe. In flouting non-intervention, Hitler was able to push appeasement further and further, openly defying international agreements he had signed, knowing that there would be no comeback from Britain. Germany also had interests in Spain, including iron ore and minerals vital to its war machine. Ensuring their supply from a friendly source was a useful by-product of aiding Franco. However, one of the main purposes in German military intervention in Spain was to test men and equipment, especially in the recently created Luftwaffe.

Hermann Goering, Commissioner for Air during the Third Reich, said at the Nuremberg trials of Nazis following the Second World War,

"When the Civil War broke out in Spain, Franco sent a call for help to Germany, and asked for support, particularly in the air. One should not forget that Franco with his troops was stationed in Africa and that he could not get the troops across as the fleet was in the hands of the communists… The decisive factor was first of all to get his troops over to Spain. The Fuhrer thought the matter over. I urged him to give support under all circumstances, firstly, in order to prevent the further spread of communism in that theatre, and, secondly, to test my young Luftwaffe at this opportunity in this or that technical respect."[2]

---

2 Hermann Goering at the Nuremberg trials in Paul Preston, *The Spanish Civil War, Reaction, Revolution and Revenge*, p 153.

On 31st July 1936, a company was set up in Spanish Morocco in order to facilitate the transfer of goods to Germany as compensation for the military aid received. The company was called HISMA (*Sociedad Hispano-Marroqui de Transportes*) and was later accompanied by ROWAK (*Rohstoffe-und-Waren-Einkaufsgellschaft*), an equivalent company in Germany to try to continue to mask the truth behind Germany's intervention. Germany sent pilots as part of Operation Magic Fire who flew the German transport planes. This initial input was greatly increased as the war went on. Operation Magic Fire officially ended in October 1936 when it was replaced by/renamed Operation Guido and supplies intensified and widened to include all aspects of the German military. In the ten weeks of Operation Magic Fire's existence, 13,500 troops, 127 machine guns and 36 field guns had been carried into Spain from Morocco. By September, tanks and bombs had also been supplied by Germany and the German pilots moved from supporting, transporting and training the Nationalists to participating directly in the conflict.

Following the official recognition of Franco's regime by Germany at the end of September, there was an increase in the supplies sent to the Nationalists by Germany. As Operation Magic Fire was wound down, a new means of organising the Grman involvement emerged which was eventually named the Condor Legion. Although mainly remembered for the air force element, the Condor Legion also included army support, particularly tanks and anti-aircraft guns. The aeroplanes took part in the attack on Madrid and along with their Italian counterparts and under Franco's orders, deliberately bombed civilian areas in the city. The Germans were particularly keen to see the effects of this and many of the tactics later employed in World War Two were developed in Spain. They were part of the Nationalist forces at the battle of Jarama but the Condor Legion will forever be linked with an event a few months later, in April 1937, in the Basque market town of Guernica.

Monday, 26th April 1937 was a market day in Guernica. The place was of symbolic importance to the Basque people. The tree of Guernica was a symbol of Basque nationalism and the small market town, although not important strategically, was held in high regard by the Basque people. It had for centuries stood as the guarantor of the traditional freedoms and laws of the Basque people, a place for the lords to meet. On that Monday in April, the town's population, as always increased on market day, had been further swelled by an influx of refugees fleeing the advancing Nationalist forces. The church bells in this deeply religious, Catholic stronghold, sounded the alarm of an enemy air raid. Most went into the cellars designated for just such an event. A lone German plane flew overhead a dropped bombs on the town centre before flying off. People rushed from the shelters to help those who had been injured, when the rest of the bombing squadron flew over.

As the bombs dropped, it was clear that the flimsy cellars offered little protection and soon most were fleeing into the fields to try to escape the carnage. The planes began to bomb, grenade and use their machine guns on the women, children and livestock who were desperately trying to get away. Even the nuns from the local hospital were targeted. Almost unbelievably, the worst was yet to come. Shortly afterwards, three squadrons of the large Junkers 52 planes flew over and began to carpet bomb the town, taking over two and a half hours, flying over again and again. Carpet bombing had just been invented by the Condor Legion during the bombing of Oviedo in the Asturias. The devastation caused in Guernica was difficult to comprehend.

Then planes dropped many massive bombs which meant some families were obliterated in their houses or in the cellars they had fled to for protection. The Condor Legion also dropped anti-personnel bombs and incendiaries which lit the whole town on fire. Crazed animals, their skins burning with phosphorus, ran wildly in the streets until they died. There were hundreds of human casualties, although estimates differ wildly. The town was utterly destroyed.

The immediate aftermath of Guernica was one of horror. Reports carried in British and American newspapers brought home the utter devastation which had been wreaked and the helplessness of civilians against this new facet of modern warfare. The Nationalists tried to spin their way out of it, initially claiming that the town had been destroyed by retreating Republicans but few except ardent supporters could hold on to that fabrication for long. It is certainly clear now that this symbol of Basque nationalism was used a testing ground for a new type of warfare and one that terrified the civilian populations of Britain. The prophesy that Stanley Baldwin had made in 1932 that, "The bomber will always get through" had never seemed so chillingly apt.

Not only were the fortunes of the Nationalists inexorably linked to the intervention of Italy and Germany, Franco's personal triumphs were too. It is certainly true that he benefitted from the deaths of Sotelo, Sanjurjo, Goded, Fanjul, Jose Primo de Rivera and - in June 1937 – Mola: leaving Franco with few rivals. He had become leader of the military campaign of the Nationalists because he led the Army of Africa and because all of the Italian and German aid was channelled through him. He was able to take advantage of his good fortune as his rivals died because of the position of strength that the Axis aid gave him. The Nationalists were able to call on virtually unlimited supplies of new men and machinery that the Republicans could simply not replace. The scale of the Italian intervention and the increasingly sophisticated nature of the German contribution tipped the scales overwhelmingly in the Nationalists favour and ensured they won. That Germany and Italy should want to enable a fellow fascist to be victorious is perhaps unsurprising; it is less obvious why Britain would allow them to do so.

The truth is that Spain was another tragic victim of the policy of appeasement, allowing Mussolini and Hitler to do virtually whatever they wanted without reprisal and only stern words - without force behind them - in reprimand. Abyssinia, Austria and Czechoslovakia were to meet a similar fate as Spain, sacrificed on the false alter of peace. What has been labelled, "The Spanish Tragedy" occurred with the acquiescence and effect support of both the British Government and for the most part, Churchill.

11
POSITION NO. 3 'THE SUPREME FARCE OF OUR TIME'

It is difficult to say exactly when Churchill began to feel uneasy about the policy of non-intervention. Initially the proposal met with widespread support. It provided a get-out for a beleaguered French government; a continuation of appeasement for the British; a relief for the Labour leaders who had faced pressure to demand active support of the Republic; and one less possible trapdoor into war for most of the British people. It did seem to fly in the face of international convention however, as it set the elected Government of Spain on an equal footing with the rebel generals. It denied normal belligerent rights to the Republic to purchase arms with which to defend itself and its people. However, from a British perspective, it meant that there was no chance of Britain becoming involved in another war because of something that was happening in a distant land with seemingly no direct link to Britain itself. For British commercial interests, non-intervention also meant that British companies should not be disadvantaged should the side their government backed lose. For many Conservatives, non-intervention provided a means to support the Nationalists while appearing to be neutral.

Churchill certainly continued to voice his approval well after the policy was shown to be flawed in the extreme. Although Germany and Italy had signed up to the pact, as we have seen above, the rate at which they supplied the Nationalists with men and equipment continued to grow unabated. In January

1937, Churchill wrote that "Everything that has happened since (British adoption of the policy of non-intervention) justifies and strengthens that policy."[1] He explained this with three arguments. The first reason was that Spain was now evenly divided both in terms of the land held and armed forces. This was approximately true at that point in the war, if the German and Italian presence is ignored. The initial push by the Nationalists, from both north and south, to take Madrid had failed. The war continued on other fronts, in Aragon and elsewhere, but there was a more settled look to the map of Spain at the beginning of 1937, although as the amount of materiel from the Axis powers mounted, this was to change.

Secondly, Churchill argued, "Both sides have sullied their conflicting causes with unspeakable cruelties."[2] By this time, as had been the case for some months, the atrocities were almost wholly one-sided and carried out by the Nationalists. This was partly because it was Franco and Mola's who were advancing in the autumn and winter and so it was the Nationalist forces who were taking over new territory with populations who had previously been under Republican control. The Republican reprisals against the vested interests of the Church, large landowners, capitalists and prominent right-wingers had almost all happened in the early days and for the most part was spontaneous. As the Nationalists gained ground, they had more opportunity to commit outrages against individuals and groups. However, this does not tell the whole story. The Nationalists used terror against the civilian population as an instrument of war. If Franco was correct that he was liberating Spain, then the advancing Nationalist forces should have been met with open arms by the newly "freed" people. This was not the case and instead in every area that the Nationalists won by force, the local

---

1 Winston Churchill in *No Intervention in Spain* in *Step by Step*, p 83.
2 *Ibid.* p 83.

Position No. 3: 'The Supreme Farce of Our Time'

population suffered executions, torture, rape and brutality. The streams of refugees were almost all in one direction, away from the Nationalists and into what they hoped would be the safety of the Republican areas.

The third reason Churchill gave for maintaining the non-intervention policy was that, "neither side in any way represents the British point of view."[3] By that he really meant the British Conservative point of view, but he wanted to couch it in such terms as making out as if the fight were between "Nazi dictators or Bolshevik dictators".[4] This was not new from Churchill of course but was once again tragically incorrect. Churchill stated that he desired "to see the return of a liberal age where Parliaments will guard freedom"[5] which of course was exactly what the Republican governments had been doing until they were attacked by elements of their own army. Since 1931, Spain had created a modern, liberal constitution, rolled back some of the stranglehold of the Church, implemented modest agrarian reforms, introduced universal adult suffrage, held three democratic multi-party elections, put down attempted risings from Left and Right and improved the lives of many of its citizens. This is exactly the type of country that Churchill should have been standing up for, but unfortunately his inability to distinguish between democratic socialists (or even left leaning Liberals) and Bolshevists led to his blinkered view.

Churchill also spoke of "volunteer soldiers, weapons and munitions which Germany and Italy are sending to General Franco".[6] By this time it was abundantly clear that the Italian soldiers fighting in Spain for the Nationalists were not spontaneous volunteers, but conscripts sent by Mussolini. It is true that there were dedicated fascists who also travelled but

---

3 *Ibid.* p 83.
4 *Ibid.* p 84.
5 *Ibid.* p 84.
6 *Ibid.* p 83.

they did so in Italian military ships and aircraft, supplied with Italian military equipment and fought using Italian military guns and ammunition. There was no hiding the overt nature of the weapons supplied by Germany and Italy by 1937, for Churchill to try to pretend otherwise was untenable. Indeed, later in the same article, Churchill stated that it was argued by those who support British intervention "that if General Franco wins with the help of the Nazi and Italian dictators, Spain will be a new focus of Nazi tyranny and power."[7] Churchill is acknowledging the direct intervention of Germany and Italy, even though he then goes on to suggest that if Franco wins, every Spaniard will then just want to push the Germans and Italians out (as if the people would suddenly unite). Churchill also dismisses any fear that this could endanger France, leaving it menaced on three sides. Churchill rather incredulously believed that, "It does not, however, follow that if General Franco wins he will be grateful to his Nazi and Fascist allies."[8]

Churchill also reiterated another argument put forward in favour of non-intervention, that seeming neutrality by Britain would help ensure that Spain "would like to live on extremely friendly terms (with Britain)."[9] It may seem strange now that anyone thought that whichever side won in Spain they would be more friendly towards a country that had not helped them than to one which had, however that is the argument that Churchill (and not only him) put forward. Non-intervention was seen as hedging one's bets against either outcome, however this ignored both that intervention by Britain on the side of the Republic would make it more likely that the Republic would win; and that any emergent regime would naturally be on friendlier terms with the countries who had helped it prevail. This also

---

7 *Ibid.* p 84.
8 *Ibid.* p 84.
9 *Ibid.* p 84.

Position No. 3: 'The Supreme Farce of Our Time'

misunderstands that not only would British intervention have made a Republican victory more likely through strength of arms, but it would have deterred Italy and probably Germany from intervening. Mussolini waited until he knew what the British reaction was going to be before he committed to send aid to Franco. Hitler too, just months before the outbreak of war in Spain, had sweated over British and French reaction to his occupation of the Rhineland, knowing that any show of strength would mean he would have had to retreat.

It is worth noting that those advocating British intervention were not suggesting that there should be any troops sent. At the most basic level, they were arguing that the Spanish Republic should be allowed to buy weapons and equipment from Britain. If Britain had declared the Republican government to be the only legitimate one in Spain and that the actions of the Generals was an anti-democratic insurgency, then they could have paved the way for the Republic to buy means with which to defend itself and most likely triumph. If this had also led to a lack of involvement on behalf of the Nationalists by Italy and Germany, then a Republican victory would have been certain.

Churchill had another motive in writing the article in January 1937. As usual, he was trying to convince a British public inclined to be largely sympathetic towards the Republic, that each side was as bad as the other so we should stay well clear. However, he was also reacting to rumours that there were rumblings with the British Government about the efficacy of non-intervention. The British Government were uneasy about the level of intervention in Spain by Italy and Germany and even more upset about loses to British shipping in the Mediterranean due to Italian naval action. There was no real chance of Britain abandoning the policy in January 1937, this was over a year before foreign secretary Anthony Eden would resign over the government's courting of Italy. However, Churchill was concerned enough to write that it disturbs him "when I read that we have sent 'sharp notes' and have delivered 'emphatic protests'".[10] "We should adhere obstinately to our neutrality and (avoid) however tempting... partisanship."[11] This is Churchill, in 1937, not only supporting the British Government's policy of appeasement but chastising them for even protesting to Germany and Italy about military intervention in a foreign country.

There had been some changes by the time Churchill next returned to the subject of the Spanish conflict at the beginning of April less than three months later, but not much had altered in Churchill's thinking. The changes were not in his blinkered view of the atrocities which were being committed. Churchill thunders against outrages of Red Terror in Malaga and although he states that, "no one can doubt that grim retaliation has been practised by the Nationalist Government"[12] his account of what happened in Malaga is perverse. It is true that in reprisal for the bombing of civilian areas, a number of Nationalist hostages held on a prison ship were killed by sailors' committees. However, the slaughter of almost 4000 unarmed civilians and prisoners by the Nationalists once they had taken the city was on scale that is difficult to imagine. The Nationalists then bombed and shelled the lines of refugees from the city as they fled along the coast. Thousands of civilians died in this 'caravan of the dead'. There is no doubt that Churchill was receiving very biased and pro-Nationalist information on the situation in Spain, as the British Government were too. It is also clear though that Churchill only chose to pay heed to those reports which fitted his global view.

Churchill's views on non-intervention at this time show some realisation of the "supreme farce of our time" as Nehru dubbed it but also a breathtaking naivety on his part. Churchill

---

10 *Ibid.* p 85.
11 *Ibid.* p 85.
12 Winston Churchill, *Can the Powers bring Peace to Spain?* in *Step by Step*, p 108.

Position No. 3: 'The Supreme Farce of Our Time'

notes that "In spite of all the fraud and humbug which has brought derision upon Mr Eden's Non-Intervention Committee, it has still presided over a considerable limitation of foreign intervention in Spain."[13] This acknowledges there was some lack of effectiveness but overestimates any good it had done. Eden himself said that "a leaky damn is better than no damn at all" but both he and Churchill were being less than honest. There was no restraint whatsoever in Italian men, equipment and munitions reaching the Nationalists. They had the whole of the Mediterranean to use to transport the aid. Italian ships and submarines were also used to sink any vessel they suspected of taking supplies to the Republic, including British shipping. Churchill states in this article that the Italians are cooperating in a blockade, but he cannot have been that gullible as to believe their actions were anything other than partisan. In fact, the Non-Intervention committee allowed the Italians to sink ships and lent an authority to Italy's support of the Nationalists. This was not just non-intervention aiding the Nationalists by omission but overtly.

Churchill also displayed his anti-communist bias and his naivety in the article when he stated that he believed that if Franco won, "The liberal nations (Britain and France) should be able to mitigate the severities to the vanquished of a Nationalist victory – triumph it cannot be."[14] It is not just with hindsight, with the knowledge of the thousands murdered by Franco's regime after his victory, that criticism can be made of Churchill's belief. There was ample evidence of the atrocities already committed to the people on the land 'conquered' by Franco in the war up to that point. In contrast, Churchill thought that "the success of the Anarchist and Trotskyite forces… would be followed by class and party atrocities which would… devastate and depopulate

---

13 *Ibid.* p 107.
14 *Ibid.* p 108.

the whole Iberian Peninsula."¹⁵ Again this shows complete misunderstanding of the political situation within Republican Spain. The Communists were gaining more influence at the expense of those mentioned by Churchill. Just a month after this article, in Barcelona, days of tension, unrest and fighting between the Anarchists and POUM on one side and the Communists and Republican leaders on the other saw the Communists gain even greater control. This led to the resignation of Largo Caballero as Prime Minister and his replacement by Negrín, who was much more inclined to bend towards the will of the Communist advisers and Soviet policy. This led to the absolute persecution of the POUM and to a lesser extent the Anarchists. When Churchill wrote the article, there was not a chance that a Republican win would bring about control by the Anarchists and Trotskyists.

Having recognised the criticisms of non-intervention, though not yet condemning it, Churchill also indicated toward the end of the article that his desired outcome was now that there could be "some kind of concordat in Spain, which would prevent the triumph of either side... some compromise."[16] This does mark a shift of sorts and although the article shows the contradictions and typical preoccupations of Churchill, there is an uneasiness in his writing.

Writing again at the beginning of October 1937, Churchill reflected on the recent meeting between Hitler and Mussolini and regarded it generally favourably. The Nyon conference had also met less than a month before in order to try to prevent the sinking of shipping, a lot of it British, in the Mediterranean. Much of this had been sunk by what Churchill refers to as 'pirate' submarines but of course they were from the Italian navy. The solution of the Nyon conference was to have Italy police this. Churchill actually states that, "Britain, France and Italy should be closely

---

15 *Ibid.* p 108.
16 *Ibid.* p 109.

Position No. 3: 'The Supreme Farce of Our Time'

associated in the solution of any difficulties which may arise out of the Spanish Civil War."[17] Those difficulties – the sinking of British and other ships – were caused by Italy and yet Mussolini was allowed to become a full partner in the solution. Italy's way round this was to give the submarines to Franco to become part of the Nationalist navy and so continue the blockade.

Churchill also thought that the time was coming in Spain when the fighting men on both sides would "come together on the basis of throwing out the foreign interlopers."[18] This was wishful thinking in the extreme. The Nationalists were completely dependent on Germany and Italy to replace lost men and materiel. There was no chance of Franco getting rid of the Axis powers before the war was won. With a complete lack of awareness in the same article, Churchill goes on to write about Germany and Italy's reaction to Japanese aggression in China and in particular "the wholescale massacre of helpless coolies and poor toiling fishermen by air-bombing of non-combatants."[19] He expressed his wish that Hitler and Mussolini should invite the Western democracies to join with them to bring this to an end. The increasing slaughter wrought by the Japanese on civilians, such as the Nanking massacre in December 1937, which left up to 300 000 dead was clearly appalling, not to say embarrassing for Churchill, who had been an apologist for the Japanese. As one biographer states, "Churchill's defence of Japanese militarism then looked extremely ill-advised and he simply chose to ignore what had happened in Nanking."[20] Even when criticising the bombing of 'helpless coolies', Churchill fails to make the connection between the actions of the Japanese and the aerial bombing of civilians that had been carried out by Germany and Italy for well over a year by this point. Guernica (see chapter 10)

---

17 Winston Churchill, *The Dictators have Smiled* in *Step by Step*, p 161.
18 *Ibid.* p 162.
19 *Ibid.* p 162.
20 Anthony Tucker-Jones, *Churchill Master and Commander*, p 131.

had happened less than six months previously.

When Churchill turned again to Spain at the end of November 1937, his altering approach can be seen. Although he raises some of his familiar tropes, he recognises that "It is... wrong to call the Valencian and Catalonian Governments[21] a mob of savage Bolsheviks",[22] despite this being exactly what he has been calling them. Churchill believed at this time that Spain's road to peace was the "restoration of a constitutional monarchy."[23] Ignoring that Spain had previously had a monarch who appointed dictators and therefore could hardly be said to have been a constitutional one in any recognisable sense, this does mark a shift. Envisaging a Spain in which Franco is not the leader and shows Churchill's growing uneasiness that another dictatorship may occur in Europe, established with the help of Hitler and Mussolini.

Churchill's review of the year written near the end of 1937 shows his realisation that the intervention in Spain by Germany and Italy should be regarded as worrying from a British point of view. "While promising solemnly and repeatedly not to intervene, the German and Italian Dictators have thrown their weight in on one side."[24] In the same document, Churchill acknowledged that the Italian troops fighting in Spain were sent by Mussolini, "the Italian dictator having also sent a considerable army to Spain.."[25] This acknowledgement that non-intervention had failed and was leading to a probable Nationalist victory was then Churchill's third position on the Spanish conflict. In Spain itself in December 1937, the Republicans launched a massive attack on Nationalist positions at Teruel in Aragon. This saw

---

21 Republican Spain's official Government were in Valencia while their northern stronghold was the Catalan devolved Government in Barcelona.
22 Winston Churchill, *Spain's Road to Peace* in *Step by Step*, p 178.
23 Ibid. p 178.
24 Winston Churchill, *Panorama of 1937* in *Step by Step*, p 186.
25 Ibid. p 187.

the Republic gain territory and eventually capture the city of Teruel by early January. In Spain's worst winter for decades, the two armies fought through snow, with frostbite causing many casualties. By the end of February however, the Nationalist counter offensive had retaken the city and gained more ground to the north. The constant supply of German and Italian planes proved too much for the Republican air force which was decimated. Unlike their counterparts, the Republicans could not replace the lost machines. The Aragon area was now open to a Nationalist advance and by the end of April 1938, Republican Spain was cut in two as the Nationalists reached the coast. It was the beginning of the end.

12
SOVIET UNION AID - A HELP AND A HINDERANCE

The support given by the Soviet Union for the Spanish Republic ensured that there was no Nationalist victory in 1936 and saved Madrid from Franco's attempts to take the capital. From the outset, Soviet aid was controversial and as the war wore on, its efficacy was questioned. Certainly, in hindsight there has been doubt cast as to whether overall the assistance given by the Soviet Union was worth the price paid by the Republic.

From the outset, the Spanish Communists sought to collaborate with the other Republican forces in defeating the generals' attempted coup. This was in line with the Comintern's position which had seen them join the Popular Front to fight the election. One of the reasons for this was to ensure that the outside world saw the fight as between an independent, democratic Spanish Republic and international fascism. In keeping with this (as well as ideological opposition to a proletarian revolution which was not controlled by them), the Communists were keen to show that there was no revolution in Spain by the Left; but also, no chance of Spain becoming a satellite communist state beholden to the Soviet Union. Not only did Stalin believe that this was the best chance of survival for Republican Spain, he also – and far more importantly for him – wanted to be on the same side as Britain and France. If Spain were involved in a defence of democracy against the German and Italian dictators, it would draw the Soviet Union closer to Britain and France.

What decided the Soviet Union to escalate its support from encouraging the Spanish Communists to back the Republic to actively supplying weapons, was the intervention of Germany and Italy. By late August of 1936, the supplies from the Axis powers threatened to bring a swift end to the conflict in Spain in favour of the Nationalists. Reports from Spain, some via the French Communists, spoke of the perilous state of the Republic, with no regular army and a fragmented chain of command. Above all they stated that what the Republic needed, if it was to halt the seemingly unstoppable advance of the Nationalists, was weapons. Towards the end of September, Stalin approved the supply of nearly 100 T-26 tanks and a smaller number of fighter planes.

One of the effects of the aid was to boost the profile and importance of the PCE. The Spanish Communist Party had been a very junior member of the Popular Front, and its membership was under 40 000 before the outbreak of the civil War. The recognition of support from the Soviet Union led to an upsurge in good feeling towards both the country and the Party who were effectively its Spanish representatives. Membership of the PCE soared to 200 000 by the end of 1936 and another 100 000 were added to this by the end of March.[1] This helped to change the balance within the Republican government. The Communists gained more influence within the government, although this had started from the inclusion of two PCE members in Caballero's broad-based cabinet in September 1936, which also included anarchists. The influence of the Party was also felt within the military. The reorganisation to create the new People's army, began in October 1936 and continued until completion in 1937, was very heavily influenced by Soviet advisors and policy (see below). Caballero, despite having been called "The Spanish Lenin" by Pravda, remained one step removed from the Communist influence and fiercely independent. He often clashed with attempts to dictate policy directly to him by Soviet

---

1 Antony Beevor, *The Battle for Spain*, p 150.

Soviet Union Aid - A Help and a Hinderance

advisors. The Soviet ambassador, Marcel Rosenberg, took to visiting Caballero on a daily basis, accompanied by the Spanish Foreign Minister, Alvarez del Vayo, who acted as translator. Although in great need and therefore forced to tolerate these constant meetings, Caballero's patience eventually snapped on one infamous occasion, when he roared at Rosenberg to

"Get out! Get out! You will have to learn, Senor Ambassador, that although we Spaniards are very poor and need help from abroad very much, we are too proud to let a foreign ambassador attempt to impose his will on the head of the government of Spain! And as for you, Vayo, it would be better to remember that you are a Spaniard and Minister of Foreign Affairs of the Republic and that you should not combine with a foreign diplomat in putting pressure on your Prime Minister."[2]

The Communists eventually got a Spanish Prime Minister who was more willing to dance to their tune when Caballero was forced to resign in May 1937 following the events in Barcelona earlier that month, and Negrín took his place. Trouble had been brewing in the Catalan capital for some time. The communists, liberal Republicans and moderate PSOE members were seeking to wrest back control of governance of the area from the anarchists, POUM and revolutionary elements of the PSOE who had seized control in the aftermath of the defeat of the generals' rising. The argument of those who wanted to downplay the revolutionary nature of Catalonia and Aragon was that removing people such as Andreu Nin (POUM leader who had been Minister of Justice in the Catalan *Generalitat* until December 1936) was showing to Britain and France that the Spanish Republic was a moderate place and not revolutionary, thus making these countries more likely to offer support. By May 1937 however, it seemed clear that this tactic was not working as Britain in particular showed no

---

2 Quoted in Paul Preston, *The Spanish Civil War: Reaction, Revolution and Revenge*, p 251.

inclination whatsoever to help the Republic. As the *Generalitat* tried to take back control from the revolutionary trade unions, tensions increased further. All of this was not helped by food shortages and increased population in Barcelona due to an influx of refugees. When the *Generalitat* called for all trade union groups to surrender their weapons and leave policing to the authorities in March 1937, the anarchists resigned from the government of the *Generalitat*. Concerned that the traditional May Day celebrations could get out of control, the *Generalitat* cancelled them, but this only infuriated the anarchists and others further.

On 3rd May, there was a raid on the CNT controlled telephone exchange in Barcelona by the Catalan police, led by a local communist. This was the spark which ignited the powder keg of tension which had been growing over the previous three months in particular. Barricades were erected which led to a tense stand-off, lasting for several days. The anarchists eventually stood down and told their supporters in the street to lay down their weapons and dismantle the barricades. This was largely done for the greater good. For the anarchists to properly confront the Republic's police in Barcelona, they would have to have withdrawn their forces facing Franco's troops on the front line. Ultimately, they were not prepared to do this and so backed off from further confrontation.

There were several consequences of the events of May 1937 in Barcelona. One was that Largo Caballero resigned as Prime Minister, to be replaced by Dr Juan Negrín. This suited the communists much better. There were a number of arrests of anarchists and POUM members in the immediate aftermath however of longer-term consequence politically was the scapegoating and persecution of the POUM. The POUM had already denounced the show trials in the Soviet Union, outraging the Spanish Communists and embarrassing the Soviet advisors.

NKVD (Russian secret police) agents kidnapped, tortured and killed Andreu Nin, leader of the POUM and clumsily tried to blame it on an attempted rescue by Nazis of a closet fascist. Although this was an outrage, it was not repeated on any scale and there was genuine justice in subsequent trials of those anarchists and POUM who had taken part in the May days. Moderating elements within Negrín's government, particularly Minister of Justice, Manuel Irujo, ensured that there would be no repeat of the Moscow show trials in Spain.

Another criticism of the aid sent by the Soviet Union is that it was used in a partisan way. The allegation is that the Spanish communists tended to keep the best equipment for themselves. Even if this was not true (and there is certainly some evidence for it), the aid was perceived to be used like this, which then affected behaviour. Some regimental commanders joined the Communist Party in order to ensure that they received the equipment they needed. Orwell, fighting with the POUM militia, complained that they had poorer uniforms, food and less ammunition than regular army units because of sectarian distribution of resources. However, one of the main influences of the increased prominence of the communists within the Republican military was the absorption of all of the disparate fighting groups into a unified army. The militia system had been viewed as a principal reason for the disaster at Malaga and most accepted the need for a more centralised command structure.

The increasing influence of Soviet advisors was a prominent feature of the "communisation" of the Republic and was a direct result of the aid provided. Soviet advisors were attached to all branches of the Spanish Republican military. This was necessary because of the equipment supplied, especially the tanks and planes. These had to be operated by Soviet personnel until they could train their Spanish counterparts. This was similar to the way that Germany supplied equipment and men to the Nationalists. At most there were just over 2000 Russians in Spain over the course of the war and of these over a quarter were non-combatants such as interpreters. There was a clear directive to Soviet officers not to get within range of Nationalist guns as they did not want anyone captured who could be paraded in front of the Non-Intervention committee as evidence of Russian involvement.

One of the tasks of the of the Soviet naval advisors who were present was to plot and navigate the passage of supply ships bringing the aid. Geography, in terms of both the physical and political maps of Europe was stacked against successful delivery. The border controls of fascist states and other dictatorships which abounded in central and Eastern Europe meant that it was impossible to send anything by land. The normal route for ships was via the Black Sea, through the Dardanelles into the Aegean then into the treacherous Mediterranean, where Italian ships and submarines were waiting to sink them. The difficulty in transporting aid is often underplayed when considering the amount of support that was given by the Soviet Union to the Republic. The Italians and Germans faced virtually no problems in moving their men and equipment, being within flying distance and having easy access by sea, in addition to the friendly border with Portugal. Under the corporatist state of Salazar, Portugal supported Franco and the Nationalists throughout the war. The Soviets faced immense challenges compared to the ease with which Germany and Italy could supply the Nationalists. Of the Republic's other potential allies, only Mexico gave substantial aid over the course of the war. Mexico supplied thousands of rifles and ammunition as well as acting as an intermediary for the Republic to purchase from other sources however Mexico faced great difficulty in getting these supplies across the Atlantic in the face of international opposition. France, with a common border, was ideally placed and although the border opened at different times during the conflict to allow vital supplies to reach the Republic, it was closed more often than not due to non-intervention.

The placing of Soviet advisors with regular army units caused some tension. Partly this was a clash of cultures. The Russians were not used to working with people in different political parties or with people questioning the orthodoxy of Stalinist ideology. There were also not used to alcohol being available with every meal, including during the working day. While this horrified some, others took advantage of it and had to be disciplined. Some advisors no doubt overstepped the mark when it came to their position and made demands of Spanish commanders, causing friction. Although there were some Soviets who were very experienced and brought this to Spain much to the benefit of the Republic, there were others who were younger and just as inexperienced as their Spanish counterparts. For some of the advisors however, the lack of discipline among many of the Spaniards and their refusal to follow central commands was infuriating to the Russians. Overall, the Soviet technicians, trainers and advisors were of benefit to the Republic and aided the war effort.

Much has been made of the varying quality of the materiel supplied by the Soviet Union. The collection of field guns from pre-revolutionary days were referred to as 'the battery of Catherine the Great' and an assortment of rifles sent were just as old, often requiring ammunition of different calibres. However, there is no doubting the state-of-the-art nature of the tanks and planes that arrived. They were superior to those supplied by Germany and Italy in 1936 and gave the Republic a tactical field advantage and initial air superiority until the new Messerschmidts arrived in 1937. Chain of supply difficulties detailed above were largely responsible for the limited amount of materiel which arrived. Comparisons with German and Italian aid are therefore not particularly relevant, however one contrast that can be made is how the Republic paid for the aid compared with the ease with which the Nationalists were able to be supplied almost entirely on credit, by the Italians in particular.

One of the most controversial aspects of the relationship between the Republic and the Soviet Union is the means by which the arms were purchased. From the outset of the conflict, the Spanish Republic paid for weapons with its gold reserve. It was Giral in July 1936, only a week after the start of the attempted coup, who first transferred gold to France and throughout the course of the war, over a quarter of Spain's considerable reserves were sent to Paris. In September 1936, the rest of the gold and silver was sent to Moscow for safekeeping and effectively to act as bank account for the payment of arms. This was used up through the supply of military aid and personnel. Much has been made of the exchange rates used, being favourable to the Soviet Union, and it is almost certain that regardless of the war's outcome, none of the precious metal would ever have been repatriated. In the 1950s, the Soviet Union stated that Spain still owed money.

As the war progressed and the Soviets came to have greater command of the army, their fear of failure in the eyes of the Kremlin drove them to playdown loses and not admit when events were going well. This need to show success also led to decisions to attack when a purely defensive position may have earned them more time at the very least. The battle of the Ebro is a good example of this. By the summer of 1938, Negrín's only chance of survival for the beleaguered Republic lay in holding out long enough that a European war would break out. With the brewing Czech crisis, this seemed a distinct possibility. Tentative attempts at finding a negotiated peace had failed but a war of continued resistance looked likely to be able to hold off the Nationalists for some time. The Republic were in a better position to do so since the French border had opened between

March and June allowing 18 000 tons of war materiel to cross. This replenished some of the planes and machine guns lost at the Battle of Teruel and the subsequent collapse of the Aragon front. There was still a shortage of rifles however and not enough to go round the new recruits who made up the extension of conscription to include 17-year-olds and men in their mid-forties. Artillery, anti-aircraft weapons and munitions were also in short supply. Contrary to the policy they had been pursuing, but similar to mistakes made at Brunete, Belchite and Teruel, the Republic decided to launch a large-scale offensive across the River Ebro.

The aim of the Republican attack was to cross the Ebro and try to reunite the two parts of their territory by cutting through the Nationalist's corridor to the sea. The battle followed the all too familiar pattern of previous Republican attacks. A large army of around 80 000 men was assembled for the assault. The initial crossing of the river by Republican forces on 25th July 1938, which had been well planned and rehearsed, was a success. Only near the sea was there problems, when the French XIVth International Brigade failed to get across the river in numbers and suffered very heavy casualties. By the beginning of August, the Republicans had made considerable territorial gains, reaching Gandesa, 40 kilometres from their initial position. Franco responded to the Republican advances immediately by halting his attempt to take Valencia and diverting the air power of the Nationalist, Italian and German air forces – over 300 planes - to the Ebro front.

Franco was spurred by his almost maniacal obsession that the Republic should not hold on to any ground gained. Instead of continuing his attack on Valencia, or containing the Ebro army and moving on Barcelona, Franco threw men and resources into pushing the Republic back over the Ebro and crushing their army there regardless of the cost. With almost a million men in Nationalist colours now and with an attitude towards the sacrifice of soldiers honed during his North Africa days, Franco ensured that the Battle of the Ebro was the longest and bloodiest of the war. The battle raged through the summer heat and into the Autumn, ending in the middle of November. Tens of thousands were killed, with a huge number of Republicans taken prisoner. Over 80 Republican aircraft were lost, effectively finishing the Republican air force. The Republic had also lost its army and was defeated in all but name. However, the real blow to any hope of survival had come earlier in the battle, in September. Negrín's strategy of trying to make the Spanish Civil War last long enough to be overtaken by a wider European conflict, which seemed hopeful throughout that summer, was wrecked by the surrendering of Czechoslovakia to Hitler at Munich.

Overall, the Republic could not have existed for anything like the time that it did without the support of the Soviet Union. It was also not the presence of the Russians which prevented Britain and France from supporting the Republic. The decision to implement non-intervention and treat the two sides equally was taken long before any support from the Soviets came to Spain. The aid did skew the political situation in Spain and although the centralisation of army command was probably a necessity that would have happened anyway, the persecution of the POUM and to a lesser extent the anarchists was a direct result of the influence of Moscow. The Soviet Union played one more crucial part in the Spanish Civil War though, which brought the conflict to life for much of the outside world and ensured the longevity of its appeal as an historical event: the organisation of the International Brigades.

13
THE INTERNATIONAL BRIGADES

No account of the Spanish Civil War would be complete without the inclusion of the International Brigades. This phenomenon is one of the reasons for the enduring appeal and fascination that the war has for so many. The International Brigades continue to make the Spanish Civil War local to so many people across the world because of the involvement of their countrymen and women in a foreign conflict; there are more than 100 memorials to members of the Brigades in the UK alone.

In total, more than 35 000 volunteers came from 61 different countries to support the Republic in their fight against the Nationalists. Their motives were mixed, but there are clear patterns. Over half of the volunteers were communists and many of those who travelled to Spain were displaced, from countries such as Germany and Italy. These two groups were not of course mutually exclusive. Almost all though were there to fight fascism. They recognised that the conflict mirrored the wider battle against the ideology which had forced its way to power in Italy, Germany and elsewhere.

The first foreign volunteers to aid the Republic were athletes and administrators who were attending the People's Olympiad in Barcelona. Set up as an alternative to the tarnished Berlin Olympics, several countries were represented unofficially and had just arrived when news of the attempted coup filtered through. Tensions were high in the city for a few days as the political parties and trades unions secured Barcelona for the Republic. Although many of the Olympiad participants were hastily evacuated to France, some stayed to defend the Republic and in support of the revolutionary atmosphere that was rapidly developing in the Catalan capital.

By August, many exiled Italians, Germans and Poles living in France had come south to Spain to lend volunteer. They added to those already in Spain (Italians especially) and by the end of August numbered over a 1000. The foreign volunteers at this time joined the various militias that had formed, created by political groupings, indeed there were signs at Barcelona train station pointing the way to the various recruitment centres. This steady stream now seemed to be possibly a viable source of recruits: if the spontaneous support for the Republic shown by people in many different countries could be harnessed in some military way, it could tip the balance of power in the conflict, which was now being called a civil war. This also suited Stalin and the Soviet Union. The Russian leader was very reluctant to commit any troops to Spain and although he later sent much other support (see Chapter 12), there was growing realisation that the Soviet Communists could help in another way. Buoyed by the success of the Popular Front strategy, which had seen Communist Parties in Western democracies cooperate with other progressive elements for electoral success (as had happened in Spain and France), Stalin saw another opportunity to put the Comintern network to good use.

In mid-October 1936, a delegation of Comintern officials met with the Spanish Prime Minister, Largo Caballero, with a proposal. They suggested that Brigades be established comprised of men from all countries of the world from (almost) all shades of the Left, not just communists. They optimistically said that these men would be armed themselves, so as not to be a drain on the Republic's meagre stock of weapons. Caballero listened to the proposal and agreed.

"Since you wish to fight, the Spanish Government accepts

your help, though it must be clear that you will provide your own arms. They will be paid 10 pesetas a day, the same as our own militia men."[1]

The base for the International Brigades was to be Albacete, a city in La Mancha conveniently placed for transport to most of the major places under Republican control, halfway between Madrid and the Mediterranean coast. In truth, the formal establishment of the International Brigades was only legitimising what was already happening, as groups of French, Italian, German and other nationalities had already been in Spain fighting, usually attached to various militia. British volunteers were also in Spain and, as detailed above, one early fighter to make it to Albacete was Churchill's nephew, Esmond Romilly (see Chapter 8).

The first of the International Brigades (called the XI Brigade – the five International Brigades were numbered XI – XV) marched down the Gran Via in Madrid on 8th November 1936. The Republican Government had just fled to Valencia and it seemed as if Franco's forces would take the city within hours. Foreign correspondents were already preparing articles of the capture of the Spanish capital which appeared imminent. At first the ordinary people lining the streets thought that the foreigners who marched past, giving clenched fist salutes must be Russians, but when the new troops spoke in French, German and Polish, the Madrileños and watching journalists realised they were witnessing the arrival of the most remarkable armed group of modern times.

They had arrived just in time. The very next morning, Franco's soldiers from the Army of Africa attempted to enter the city from the *Casa de Campo* park area and into the University City part of the capital. This plan however was known to the Republican commanders as it had been found on a dead Italian

---

1 Giles Tremlett, *The International Brigades*, p 65.

tank officer. The International Brigade troops were positioned to repel the attack and they, along with Sanish Republican forces, managed to do this. They had made real the cry of La Pasionaria, "No Pasarán" – they shall not pass. This was the story that the journalists in the hotels in the Gran Via had been waiting for and the legend of the International Brigades as the saviours of Madrid was born. This was an exaggeration, they fought alongside republicans from Madrid and many other parts of Spain; but it was not without foundation. They had pushed back the Nationalist forces in a brave counterattack and had helped to save the city.

A second (XIIth) International Brigade was quickly 'ordered' from Albacete and these troops were even more disparate and poorly trained than the XIth Brigade. They included Esmond Romily who travelled with the others as detailed above (see Chapter 8). The XIIth Brigade soon joined the XIth in defending the University City area of Madrid. The XIth Brigade had already suffered heavy casualties and the XIIth was to fair little better. Together though and with the ordinary citizens of Madrid, the militia columns and the loyal regular forces, they halted the Nationalist advance. The front lines established in November 1936 on the outskirts of Madrid were to change little until the very end of the war.

The Brigades were an odd mixture of experienced soldiers who had fought in World War One and totally inexperienced, often idealistic young men who were ill-prepared for battle. This affected their usefulness in a military sense. The best of them were a real asset and often much better prepared for battle than the militia and inexperienced peninsula troops who made up the rest of the Republican army. However, there were some in the International Brigades who should not have been there and others whose enthusiasm combined with a lack of combat sense meant that they did not last long when sent to the front line.

The XIIth Brigade was formed in December 1936 and took part in an ill-fated action near Teruel (almost exactly a year before the larger battle there) where many men were lost. This Brigade was a complete mix with over 20 nationalities represented, including a company from Palestine, mainly Jews. Overall, there were a large number of Jewish people from a variety of countries who joined the International Brigades to fight fascism. The example of persecution in Germany in particular, a spur. However, there was widespread antisemitism and persecution in many European countries throughout the 1920s and 1930s, one consequence of which was displacement. Another consequence was the shift leftward by many European Jews. Almost a third of the 3000+ Poles who fought in the International Brigades were Jewish (compared to around 10% of the Polish population at the time).

The influx of volunteers continued apace in the latter half of 1936. In ten weeks, 14 000 volunteers had arrived, a rate of 200 per day. In the middle of December a fourth International Brigade was raised, the XIVth Brigade in the Republican army. This included the first English speaking Company of men, mainly British and Irish (an earlier British machine gun unit's survivors became part of it too). Some ex British army officers found themselves in charge of former adversaries in IRA men. The XIVth Brigade soon saw action in the south of Spain in Andalusia. Again, many (approximately one third) of the volunteers involved in the action were lost in the fighting around Lopera just before and after Christmas.

The loses, sometimes in a chaotic manner, suffered by both the XIIIth and XIVth Brigades was taking some of the shine off of the reputation that the International Brigades had built up during their defence of Madrid. Franco was keen to expose any weakness for his own propaganda ends and displayed captured prisoners and equipment for the world's media. The lack of military experience of many of the volunteers coupled with the woefully inadequate time for training helped lead to casualty rates which were higher than should otherwise have been the case. Action in January 1937 to the northwest of Madrid saw soldiers from the XIIth and XIVth Brigades again used as shock troops and although this action brought some success in preventing the Nationalist capture of the La Coruna Road, it again came at a price. Overall, the second battle of La Coruna Road saw each side lose around 15 000 men.

Back in Albacete, more volunteers were arriving, including many from the British Isles and North America. They would soon play a part in arguably the most famous conflict of the war, the battle of Jarama. Franco's objective in February 1937 was to cross the Jarama river and cut the Madrid to Valencia road, thereby further encircling Madrid and cutting communications between there and the Republican Government in Valencia. The remnants of the British company from the XIVth Brigade and the new recruits formed the British Battalion of the XVth Brigade. They were joined in this new Brigade by another French Battalion (6th February); the Dimitrov Battalion, made up of mainly Yugoslavs and Bulgarians; and the American Abraham Lincoln Battalion.

On 12th February, the British Battalion fought over an elevated area which became known as Suicide Hill. Outnumbered around 4 to 1 (400 men faced 1600 from the Army of Africa) they struggled to maintain their position, especially as initially they had the wrong ammunition for their machine guns. Very late in the day, the correct ammunition arrived allowing them to hold the hill for that night at least. This came at a cost. "After just eight hours of fighting, the British Battalion had been reduced to half strength."[2]

The next day was to bring another blow to the British

---

2 Giles Tremlett, *The International Brigades*, p 222.

Battalion when a machine gun company was captured. At first the Moroccan Nationalist troops thought they had taken Russians prisoner (there were no Russian troops) and lined the men up. Two men, John Stevens from London and Phil Elias from Leeds were shot when Elias reached for his tobacco tin. The company second in command, Ted Dickinson complained about the shooting. James Maley from Glasgow, one of the captured men who survived, explained what happened next, "the two Spanish soldiers on either side stepped forward and blew his brains out." When it was established that the captured men were British, the executions stopped. Maley explains, "I think that's what saved us, that we happened just to be British."[3]

By 19th February, the three battalions of the XVth Brigade that had been in the front line, the British, French and Yugoslav/Bulgarian had been reduced in number by a third, but by displaying remarkable courage and along with their Spanish Republican comrades, they had halted the advance of the Nationalists and held the Madrid to Valencia road. This had come about, in part, when Frank Ryan, an Irish volunteer rallied men at the farm building called the cookhouse and led them back into the frontlines along with stragglers found along the way, by singing the world-renowned workers' anthem, "The Internationale". This was an heroic act, almost too good to be true, but there are too many eyewitness accounts for it to be apocryphal. There were numerous occasions however when enemy troops, particularly from the Army of Africa could approach Republican lines unmolested by whistling the tune of the Internationale before pouncing on the defending troops who thought they were allies. The XVth Brigade badly needed reinforcements however and they called up their reserve force, the American Abraham Lincoln Battalion.

The make-up of the American contingent was interesting.

---

3 James Maley in Willy Maley (Ed.), *Our Fathers Fought Franco*, p 36.

Generally younger than many of their European comrades and also more likely to be ollege students. Around 20% were Jewish though some estimates put this higher. Most had no military experience and their training had been basic. Losses were high, particularly after some near suicidal attempts at a counter offensive towards the end of February which saw the Lincolns lose many men. The Battle of Jarama petered out with both sides having lost heavily. The Republic's loses were mainly in the International Brigades, and both the British and Abraham Lincoln Battalions suffered greatly. Jarama was viewed as halting fascism, as had happened a few months earlier in Madrid. This had been achieved through the use of international volunteers and because many were from the British Isles and North America, the world's media took more notice. In Spain, the fighting turned to the other side of Madrid, where yet again the actions of the International Brigades would prove decisive.

Guadalajara's strategic importance and the effect that it had on Mussolini and Italian intervention in the war are discussed in Chapter 10. In the context of the International Brigades, the battle is significant because of the intervention of the Garabaldi Battalion. Part of the XIIth Brigade, the Garabaldi Battalion had been formed as early as October 1936 and had distinguished itself in the defence of Madrid. Also participating in the Battle of Jarama, the Garabaldi soldiers were resting in early March 1937 when the Nationalists launched an offensive at Guadalajara, some 70 kilometres Northeast of Madrid. The Italian volunteers in the Garabaldi Battalion knew they would be facing their countrymen, the Italian soldiers in the CTV, largely conscripts, though also containing Blackshirt Divisions. These were fascist militia, though in reality many were illiterate peasants grateful of a steady income and the false promise of a better future.

The start of this Nationalist offensive did not look

promising for the 5000 men making up the long Republican line. They were outnumbered by over 6 to 1 initially (in total in the battle, over 35 000 Italian troops were available with another 15000 Spanish Nationalist troops against 20 000 Republicans once they had been reinforced). The Italians had their own airforce, tanks, armoured vehicles and artillery pieces. From the 8th to the 11th of March, the Nationalists advanced, though not as rapidly as they would have liked. They met fierce resistance from the XIth and XIIth International Brigades, including from the Garibaldi Battalion, who shouted across no-man's land for their countrymen to come and join them. They were also slowed by the manoeuvrability of the Russian T26 tanks, which proved to be superior to anything the Nationalists possessed.

On 12th March, the Republicans launched a counter offensive. This continued for 11 days, and the Republicans routed the Italians, capturing much equipment left behind in haste by the fleeing Nationalists. The Republicans were greatly aided by having superior air support with slightly more in number but also better planes, supplied by the Soviet Union. Crucially, the Republic also had the airport at Albacete, with its concrete runway, while the Italian aircraft were bogged down in muddy fields, like many of their heavy tanks.

The Garibaldi Battalion had won their mini-Italian civil war. Over 1000 Nationalists had been taken prisoner and more than 4000 killed. It seemed like a turning point in the war. After the Republican successes in halting Nationalist attacks in Madrid, the Corunna Road and Jarama which had ended in stalemates, this was a clear Republican victory. It was not the turning point that the Republic hoped it might be however as the Italians and Germans committed more men and better equipment, as detailed previously.

The International Brigades took part in many other battles in the war. In July 1937, they were heavily involved in the Battle of Brunete, when a large Republican force attacked Nationalists laying siege to Madrid around 25 kilometres to the West of the capital. Initially successful, the Republicans were driven back and although their finishing position showed a gain of ground, it came at a heavy price. Close to 100 aircraft were lost, which the Republic found difficult to replace, along with over 10 000 men killed or wounded. Among the dead was Oliver Law, commander of the Abraham Lincoln Battalion and the first African American man to command white American soldiers. This battle also saw German International Brigaders in direct conflict with Nazi German soldiers. The latter's shouts of "Heil Hitler" were met with responses of "Death to Hitler" from the opposite front line just a couple of hundred metres away.

The Brigades fought on the Aragon Front later in the year and in December 1937 were involved in the Battle of Teruel (see Chapter 11), although not as prominently as in previous battles. By now, the regular Spanish Republican army was better equipped to initiate an advance. In addition, there was a desire to put pressure on the non-intervention committee to show up Franco as entirely dependent on foreign forces, as it would be Italian and German men and equipment which would be the mainstay of the Nationalist army in this battle. The German speaking XIth and English speaking XVth Brigades were held in reserve as the Republicans fought a bitter battle which captured Teruel over Christmas and into the New Year. For many in the Brigades, that Christmas was best time in Spain. Having not fought for some time, their numbers were swelled by new recruits, there was a festive feast and Paul Robeson, the famous American singer, entertained the soldiers.

New Year saw the International Brigades mobilised to face a counterattack by Franco's forces as he stopped his offensive on Madrid to try to take back land lost to the Republicans. The four battalions of the XVth Brigade still included the Lincoln and British battalions but now also had a Canadian, Mackenzie-Papineau Battalion. The weather was horrendous. The Lincoln Battalion christened the place they were fighting, "The North Pole" and one in ten of the British Battalion suffered from frostbite. The battle lasted two and a half months and Republican casualties were high, among them were many members of the International Brigades. The British battalion lost a third of its men and the Canadians were also decimated.

Only a few weeks later, the XIth and XVth Brigades were again caught up, this time in the Battle of Belchite, where a massive Nationalist attack smashed through Republican defences. 45,000 men from the Army of Africa successfully attacked the Republican line defended by only 6,000 troops. Close by, 35,000 Italians from the CTV advanced against only 3,000 Republicans. The motorised advance was rapid and backed by new Stuka dive-bombers, they quickly gained ground, scattering the XIth and XVth Brigades. The difference in equipment available to both sides was now overwhelming.

The British Battalion was sent to the front line again at the end of March 1938, with disastrous results. Believing the front line to be another mile away, two columns advanced past what they thought were Republican tanks. They belonged to the CTV however and when the Italians began to decimate the British, the soldiers did not even have grenades with which to fight back. Over 100 were captured with many others killed.

The last major battle of the war, the Battle of the Ebro (See Chapter 12), saw all five of the Internationale Brigades take part. There was little hope now of achieving an outright victory against Franco. What the Republicans wanted, acknowledged by the troops, was to prevent a Nationalist victory long enough for a greater European conflict to erupt. The prospects for that happening in the summer of 1938 seemed good. In June,

Churchill was writing about the "shadows over Czechoslovakia"[4] and in early July about the "rape of Austria".[5] There seemed an inevitability about another European war, which grew as the Czech crisis deepened.

The Battle of the Ebro's initial success for the Republicans soon turned to disaster and the almost complete collapse of their armed force as a credible fighting entity. In just two days in July, the Republicans had captured 800 square kilometres of territory, advancing over and far beyond the Ebro River along a vast area. A defendable mountain range was now behind them and in July and August there was hope that they could now last long enough for the democracies in Europe to react to the growing fascist menace across the continent. In September, the retreating XVth Brigade learned that Chamberlain was flying to Berchtesgaden to surrender the Sudetenland to Hitler.

On 21st September, the Spanish Premier, Negrín, announced the immediate repatriation of all foreign volunteers. This was done in a speech to the United Nations in Geneva in an attempt to shame the democracies into demanding the same of Germany and Italy or start aiding the Republic. This was a forlorn hope. The Brigades were still involved in very bloody fighting, and many lost their lives between the announcement of withdrawal and their final repatriation at the end of October. In their farewell parade in Barcelona on the 28th of October, the Brigaders marching were overwhelmed by the good wishes, kisses and flowers from a crowd of hundreds of thousands. Dolores Ibárruri, La Pasionaria, told them,

"Today many are departing. Thousands remain, shrouded in Spanish earth, profoundly remembered by all Spaniards. Comrades of the International Brigades... you can go proudly. You are history. You are legend."

---
4 Winston Churchill, *Shadows over Czechoslovakia* 23rd June 1938 in *Step by Step*.
5 Winston Churchill, *The Rape of Austria* 6th July 1938 in *Step by Step*.

14
END OF THE CIVIL WAR AND POSITION NO. 4: TOO LITTLE, TOO LATE

By April 1938, Churchill began to realise the inherent dangers of Franco victory, brought about – as he now recognised – by the German and Italian war machines.

In "Red Sunset in Spain", Churchill believed the end was imminent for the Spanish Republic. He underestimated the resilience that saw them fight on for another year. Written before the battle of the Ebro, Churchill thought the Republic was doomed. He was also beginning to see the outcome for much of the population should Franco win. In contrast to his earlier naïve belief that "patriotic, religious and bourgeois forces… are marching to re-establish order by setting up a military dictatorship."[1] Other pronouncements about an outcome under Franco where he would come to see the benefits to, "the winning side of offering fair terms of surrender to beaten foes."[2] In contrast to his misplaced 1936 optimism for Franco, Churchill now feared, "slaughter on the battlefield, and… the severities which it is to be feared will follow the subjugation of one half of Spain by the other."[3] He also stated further that, " A long period of iron repression and aching poverty is all that lies before the Spanish people."[4] Churchill could see the brutality of Franco and

---
1 Winston Churchill, *The Spanish Tragedy* in *Step by Step*, p 38.
2 Winston Churchill, *Keep out of Spain* in *Step by Step*, p 44.
3 Winston Churchill, *Red Sunset in Spain* in *Step by Step*, p 215.
4 *Ibid.* p 216.

foresee the tragedy that would unfold under his rule.

Churchill was also now fully accepting of the direct involvement of Germany and Italy and the crucial role they were playing in Franco's victory. "Under the smashing weight of German and Italian artillery and aviation, all resistance is breaking down." Churchill illustrated the emboldenment of Italy caused by their participation in Spain and the danger that the rest of Europe faced.

"One may measure the ascendency acquired by the dictator powers by the two Italian communiques which appeared simultaneously. The first warned France in strident terms of the risks she would run in intervening in Spain and lectured her upon her responsibility to avoid a European war. The second was a statement of nearly 2000 casualties in the Italian divisions which are taking part in General Franco's present offensive; and everyone knows besides that it is German artillery and aviation which has decided this phase of the struggle. Thus, Dictator Powers may do anything; the others nothing."[5]

Churchill now realised that by doing nothing, countries had effectively aided the defeat of the Spanish Republic. More than this however, Churchill now saw that this had only resulted in the strengthening of Germany and Italy as well as the honing of their military expertise. Non-intervention had not only failed, but it had also been the instrument that had allowed the Nationalist side to win. Churchill also acknowledged that this was the preferred outcome of many Conservatives "Strong elements in the Conservative Party regard the cause of Franco as their own".[6] It had not been so long since Churchill had felt the same.

Churchill had also had to face the reality of the horrors which had been perpetrated by the Nationalists. In sharp contrast

---

5 *Ibid.* pp 215-216.
6 *Ibid.* p 217.

The End of the Civil War and Position No. 4

to his language and meaning of two years' earlier, Churchill was now admitting that, "The blackest atrocities, such as the bombing of Guernica and Barcelona, with their wholesale indiscriminate butchery of women and children, were the work of his (Franco's) allies."[7] The prospect of Germany being able to repeat this in other parts of Europe were uppermost in Churchill's mind and he even mooted the possibility of Germany using the same Spanish airfields used to bomb Barcelona to rain terror on French cities such as Toulouse.

In the final words in his piece from April 1938, Churchill showed his distance from official British Government policy. Where he had been fulsome in praise of, and four-square behind, Britain's in-action in promoting non-intervention, Churchill now lambasted the policy. "A thoroughly Nazified Spain, retaining its German nucleus, would be a cause of profound anxiety to both France and Britain. At any rate, it appears to be a matter upon which they should exert themselves, if indeed the faculty of action still resides among them."[8] What action Churchill was now advocating that Britain and France take to prevent this at this late date, is not clear. That he was pushing for action was significant, however.

Only a few days later, just how little Chamberlain was prepared to do to oppose fascist aggression was to be made clear when the British-Italian agreement - the Easter Accords – was signed on the 16th of April 1938. The negotiations for this had already been at the expense of the foreign secretary. Anthony Eden had resigned in February that year after refusing to negotiate a new agreement with Mussolini when the Italians were not abiding by the previous one regarding Italy's intervention in Spain. The continued supply of men and materiel was of little regard to Chamberlain but Eden, the man who Mussolini called,

---

7 *Ibid.*
8 *Ibid.* pp 218.

"The best dressed fool in Europe" resigned as a public protest. Under the Accords, Italy was meant to withdraw its forces from Spain but effectively Mussolini could wait until Franco's victory.

Writing about this in May, Churchill attacked the Italians for their intervention in Spain, "when whole army corps of foreign regular troops participated, contrary to solemn promises, in a civil war, and when submarines sank large numbers of vessels under the British flag."[9] This was completely opposite to his previous beliefs about Italian volunteers and mystery submarines which had begun to change before the end of 1937 (see chapter 11). All of Churchill's writing in 1938 was leading towards his fourth position on the Spanish Civil War, believing that the Republicans should have won.

Churchill returned to writing specifically about Spain at the very end of the year, on 30th December 1938. By this time, the International Brigades had left Spain and the British policy of appeasement had resulted in the betrayal of Czechoslovakia at Munich. The Czech crisis had been rumbling along for most of the year but came to a head in September. At its heart was the make-up of a country created after the first World War which contained over three million ethnic Germans of a total population of under 14 million. The Germans mainly lived in the area of Czechoslovakia closest to Germany known as the Sudetenland. Hitler supported a Sudeten Germans Peoples Party, which pressed for the area to become German. Acting on Hitler's orders in 1938, the Sudeten German Peoples Party started to cause disruption in Czechoslovakia, as a pretext for a German invasion to "restore order".

Chamberlain made the first of his three flights to meet Hitler in the middle of September 1938 and after flying back home for meetings, returned to Germany a week later believing that he had averted war. At this second meeting at Bad Godesberg,

---
9 Winston Churchill, B*ritain and Italy* in *Step by Step*, p 229.

The End of the Civil War and Position No. 4

despite Chamberlain having achieved agreement with France and others which met Hitler's demands, the German Chancellor presented new requirements. In truth, Hitler wanted to invade Czechoslovakia using the blitzkrieg tactics practised in Spain. He now demanded the immediate transfer of the Sudetenland to Germany, to be secured by German troops. Chamberlain was bewildered and left Germany fearing war. The Czechs rejected the demand and their ally, France, mobilised, as did the British Royal Navy. At the end of September, the one event which could possibly have saved the Spanish Republican Government, a wider European conflict, seemed close.

Chamberlain's flight to Munich at the end of September was for a summit, suggested by Mussolini, to which only Germany, Britain, Italy and France were invited. The Soviet Union and crucially the Czechs themselves, were not welcome. The result was the ceding of the Sudetenland without a fight and Hitler's forces marched into the Sudetenland in October; by March the rest of Czechoslovakia had been annexed. Churchill and the Labour leader, Clement Attlee both condemned the Munich agreement, for which Chamberlain was widely praised at the time. Churchill believed that Britain had been offered a choice between war and shame and chose shame but would get war. Attlee believed, "We have seen today a gallant, civilised and democratic people betrayed and handed over to ruthless despotism."[10] He was talking about the fate of Czechoslovakia, but he could equally have been talking about the tragedy of Spain.

It was against this background then that Churchill wrote, "The Spanish Ulcer" at the end of December 1938. Churchill had nailed his anti-appeasement colours to the mast when he had called the Munich agreement "a total and unmitigated

---

10 Clement Attlee, House of Commons, 3rd October 1938.

defeat"[11] and was now able to give an honest assessment of the Spanish Civil War, one which was now not blinkered by his usual preoccupations of class and anti-bolshevism. Churchill stated that:

"It must be admitted that if at this moment the Spanish Government were victorious, they would be so anxious to live on friendly terms with Great Britain, they would find so much sympathy among the British people for them, that we should probably be able to dissuade them from the vengeance which would have attended their triumph earlier in the struggle. On the other hand, if Franco won, his Nazi backers would drive him to the same kind of brutal suppressions as are practised in the Totalitarian States. The victory of the Spanish Republic would, therefore, not only be a strategic security for British Imperial communications through the Mediterranean, but gentler and reconciling forces would play a larger part."[12]

This then was the fourth position of Winston Churchill, he had gone from supporting the Nationalists and believing their cause legitimate; to backing non-intervention; to realising the farce of non-intervention; to finally recognising that it would be better, for Britain and Spain, if the Republic won. Although Churchill had believed that the war was over earlier in April, he now thought that there was some hope, "Now is the time! Now while the issue still hangs in the balance, now before the huge shadow of European antagonism further darkens the scene, now let the Spaniards come together."[13] To believe at the end of 1938 that there was to be any outcome other than a total victory for the Nationalists was naïve in the extreme.

About a week before Churchill wrote this, Franco began a massive invasion of Catalonia. The defeat at the battle of the

---

11 Winston Churchill, House of Commons, 3rd October 1938.
12 Winston Churchill, *The Spanish Ulcer* in *Step by Step*, p 300.
13 *Ibid.* p 303.

The End of the Civil War and Position No. 4

Ebro and the retreat from there had left the region virtually undefended. With no hope of reinforcements for the Republic, the motorised columns and aerial bombardment swept through Catalonia with Tarragona falling on the 15th of January 1939, with Barcelona, so long a stronghold and the target of relentless bombing, finally succumbing on the 26th.

The last days of the Spanish Republic were predictably tragic. Franco's strategy throughout the war had been to mop up all resistance, to ensure that all of an area had been subdued before moving on. This, methodical even ponderous approach had frustrated many, including his German and Italian backers. Franco though saw his conquest as similar to the Reconquista when the Christian kingdoms of Spain had defeated the Muslim ones and effectively created a united Spain. Franco believed - and wanted to project the notion that - he was ridding Spain of a foreign belief system. At the head of a holy crusade Franco portrayed himself as a liberator. While he certainly had the support of the Church, the truth was that the people he was meant to be liberating fled from his army to the precarious safety to be found behind Republican lines. By the end of February, France and the United Kingdom both officially recognised the Franco regime as the legitimate one in Spain, although the war had not yet officially ended.

The beleaguered Republican government tried to negotiate a surrender but for Franco, this was never an option. In an attempt to get more favourable terms in defeat, a faction of the Republican army, led by Colonel Casado and fronted by veteran socialist politician Julián Besteiro, rebelled against Prime Minister Negrín and the Communist influence in the leadership and military. They formed the National Defence Council in order to negotiate some form of peace settlement. Communist troops defending Madrid reacted against this new ruling Junta and a pitiful, if short lived, civil war within a civil war broke out.

All of this was in vain as Franco would accept nothing less than unconditional surrender. At the end of March, the Nationalists began their final assault and soon mopped up the last of the Republican forces. On 1st April 1939, Franco broadcast that he was now in control of all of Spain, bringing an end to the Civil War.

The war had devastated the country. In human terms, between 250 000 and 750 000 combat deaths occurred. The wide disparity in the estimates show the difficulties in obtaining exact facts from this period. After the war, Franco and his regime were not keen to publish official figures. As we shall see, the deaths continued after the official end of the conflict and many records from both the time of the war and the repression afterwards were deliberately destroyed later as Franco looked to the legacy of his rule. The war also decimated and displaced the civilian population. The air raids alone had killed up to 15 000 non-combatants. The war also caused a massive refugee problem. During the conflict many had fled the approach of the Nationalists but when the war ended and Franco was in total control, they had few other places to go. Many Republicans who had reason to fear for their lives in a Nationalist Spain, particularly those who had been in Catalonia, fled over the border to France if they could. An estimated half a million Spaniards sought refuge in France but often this was not the end of their ordeal. Tens of thousands were held in squalid conditions in camps. Some were encouraged to return to Spain, only to be interred – or worse – in the attempt to "purify" them. For some left in France, the second world war and the fall of France brought no respite to their suffering. The Republicans were now "political prisoners" and the Vichy government handed them over to the Nazis. Interred along with French Jews in the Drancy internment camp before deportation, around 5000 Spanish Republicans perished in the Mauthausen concentration camp. Others, such as former Spanish President

Largo Caballero, were held in the Sachsenhausen concentration camp, although he managed to survive the war, dying in exile in Paris in 1946.

Churchill was to write once more about Spain in the final few weeks of the civil war. In a piece called, "Hope for Spain" on 23rd February 1939, Churchill thought, rather naively, that the "lever of Recognition" could be used by Britain and France to "procure merciful treatment for the beaten side."[14] This was a forlorn hope for two reasons. Firstly, Franco had no intention of letting anyone – let alone Britain and France – tell him how he was to conduct himself within Spain. He had set out his goal clearly to destroy all vestiges of left-wing politics in Spain and if nearly three years of war had not deflected him, slight diplomatic pressure from countries who were not allies to the Nationalists would certainly not. Secondly though, Britain (especially) and France had no intention of now interfering in Spain on behalf of the beleaguered Republicans. Britain and France recognised Franco as the head of Spain just four days later, on 27th February. While hoping that Franco can now become a great leader, Churchill is acutely aware that the continent is treading water at this time until the "outcome of the European crunch"[15] as he puts it is known. He does however have a last pop at non-intervention, setting out how surprising it was that the policy "prevented the constituted Government of Spain from buying from abroad even weapons which they had ordered before the outbreak, to pay for which they had ample funds."[16] Churchill then described how non-intervention became "an elaborate system of official humbug.. (which meant) Germany and Italy have brazenly supported Franco not only with arms but with men."[17]

---

14 Winston Churchill, *Hope in Spain* in *Step by Step*, p 318.
15 *Ibid.* p 321.
16 *Ibid.* p 319.
17 *Ibid.* p 319-320.

The European crunch, as Churchill called it, was drawing ever closer. By the middle of March the rest of Czechoslovakia was lost, but the real damage to the country had been when the Sudetenland had been handed by Britain to Germany six months earlier. Mussolini wasted no time when freed from the conflict in Spain to invade Albania at the beginning of April. The future for Europe looked bleak and President Roosevelt publicly questioned Hitler and Mussolini over their intentions towards their neighbours. The responses were not encouraging. Addressing this, Churchill began to set out what would become his own policy towards Spain after becoming Prime Minister in May 1940. In "After President Roosevelt's address" written on 20th April 1939, Churchill wrote in some detail about the importance of Spain being neutral in any future (by this time seemingly inevitable) European war. Churchill reminded Spain of the benefits they had obtained by being neutral in the last war and how both sides in any future conflict would be at least equally as enriching: "a neutral Spain would be courted by the combatants."[18] Churchill feared that Franco could be "intoxicated by his success or that he is no longer a free agent to act in the true interests of his country."[19]

To most, the prospect of Spain remaining neutral in any prolonged European war, especially one that their erstwhile allies, Germany and Italy seemed to be winning, was not realistic. This however was exactly the situation faced by Churchill as Prime Minister just over a year later, however Churchill and others managed to keep Spain out of the war through a series of measures which will be outlined in the following chapters. Standing on the brink of a European war, with Germany and Italy transferring their belligerence from Spain to their neighbours as

---

18 Winston Churchill, *After President Roosevelt's Message* in *Step by Step*, p 340.
19 *Ibid.* p 340.

they expanded and unleashed their military might, Churchill could only rue the opportunity that both countries had been given on the Iberian Peninsula. They were allowed to destroy a democracy in Spain, hone their fighting skills against the Spanish Republican army and countless civilians and prove to all, not least themselves, that Britain and France would stand by to let it happen.

15
WWII - CHURCHILL BRIBES FRANCO'S GENERALS

The events of May 1940, when Churchill replaced Chamberlain as Prime Minister, have been well documented. A pivotal moment for Britain in the second World War which paved the way for the coalition National Government which was to oversee final victory. Churchill was one of the few Conservatives who would have been acceptable to Attlee and the Labour front bench and the only one among those who were considered for the post. During the course of the war, Churchill was understandably fixed on winning and so concerned himself almost exclusively with events overseas, unless the domestic issue was production of war materials or otherwise directly related to the war effort. In terms of foreign policy however, Churchill was able to expand his thoughts wider than the immediate necessity of victory and consider the post war world.

    Spain was in a desperate state at the outbreak of the wider European conflict and certainly in no position to immediately take any part in it. Franco still had security problems, both real and imagined, and continued his persecution of the Left. Labelled by Paul Preston as "The Spanish Holocaust"[1], Franco's repression was to lead to tens of thousands more deaths and created half a million refugees. Even for those on the right side of the new regime, life could be difficult. Food was often scarce, and Franco's pursuit of autarky made it considerably worse. Having been heavily supported by Germany and Italy during the war, Franco's Spain could naturally have been expected to be

---

1 Paul Preston, *The Spanish Holocaust*.

on their side during the second World War but throughout the conflict they never formally committed, although almost 50 000 Spaniards fought for Germany on the Eastern Front as the Blue Division (see Chapter 16).

The closeness of Franco and Spain to Germany, and their eagerness to enter the war on Hitler's side, varied largely in line with the perceived certainty of German victory. In much the same way as Mussolini did when he took Italy into the war only in June 1940 with the fall of France imminent and the war apparently won, Franco was closest to joining Hitler whenever Nazi conquest seemed certain. In May, 1940, when Churchill became Prime Minister, the prospect of total Nazi victory seemed close at hand. Spain joining with Germany would not just have added more weight to the Nazi war machine, it would have meant the loss of a neutral power in a strategic position in Europe: a land bridge between the Atlantic and the Mediterranean. Above this, Spain held some useful mineral and ore deposits. Although the new Prime Minister had motives totally unconnected with Spain for doing so,[2] Churchill chose the experienced Lord Hoare as Ambassador to Madrid and tasked him with a special mission, keeping Spain out of the war.

Britain in 1940 had little to offer Spain except through trade. Even before the change of Prime Minister, Britain and Spain had signed a War Trade Agreement in March 1940. This was the result of months of negotiations between the two countries, beginning in November the previous year. The agreement, from a British point of view, sought to exploit the economically dire position that Spain was in. Firstly, it greatly eased the repayment of outstanding debt that existed between the two countries. It also established a mechanism whereby payment for Spanish

---

2 Hoare was unacceptable to Attlee and his Labour colleagues as a Cabinet member and although he wanted to stay in the Air Ministry in some capacity, or be Vice Consul in India, neither of these were desired by Churchill.

goods would help reduce this debt. In addition, the agreement loaned Franco's Spain a further £2 million (worth approximately £140 million in 2023) with which to buy (British Empire) goods. No capital from either arrangement was repayable until 1942.[3]

This agreement was later widened to include an eager Portugal and a further British loan allowed Spain to buy goods from not just Britain and the British Empire, but from Portugal and theirs. This was clearly using economics as a weapon to discourage Spain from joining with Germany. Oil, coal and food (cereals in particular) were prominent in being goods that Britain could provide, and that Spain so desperately required. The reliance on British supplies, effectively free at point of delivery, was a strong factor in maintaining Spanish neutrality in 1940. Hoare was pessimistic of the chances of this neutrality lasting much longer when he first arrived in Madrid, but Churchill was already plotting a new approach. If economic bribes which helped bolster the Franco regime within Spain, by keeping the country fed and powered, were acceptable in order to try to keep the country out of the war, perhaps more direct financial inducements could secure the aim.

June 1940 was a crucial time for the battle to keep Spain out of the war. Italy had joined with Germany, jumping on to the successful Wehrmacht band wagon that had now subdued every country it had fought, with exception of Britain. Mussolini wrote to Franco, urging him to follow suit:

"I request of you, within the broad lines of your policy, moral and economic solidarity with Italy. In the new reorganisation of the Mediterranean which will result from the war, Gibraltar will be returned to Spain."[4]

Franco's Air Minister, General Yague (before his sacking),

---

3 *Hansard*, 19 March 1940, vol 358 cc1813-5.
4 Mussolini to Franco, 9 June 1940, *Documenti Diplomatici Italiana serie 9*, volume IV, p 620 (Rome 1960).

had persuaded Franco to allow Italian planes to secretly refuel on Spanish soil. Yague, before being caught out in his own intrigue, now urged Franco to join Mussolini in the war alongside Germany. Ciano, the Italian foreign Minister (and Mussolini's son-in-law) who had worked closely with the Spanish throughout the Civil War, now asked Franco to amend Spain's status from one of neutrality to that of non-belligerent. Italy had done the same prior to entering the war and the move was seen as ominous by Britain. Franco's reply to Mussolini was gushing with praise for the Italian Dictator and promised all the support for Italy that Spain could give, though Franco regretted that the current state of the army meant that the country could not, for now, join the war.

    Mussolini was delighted with the change to non-belligerent and believed (as did Britain and others) that this was a prelude to declaring war at some point in the not too distant future. Just days afterwards, as the Nazis occupied Paris, on the 14th of June, Franco moved his troops into the Tangier International zone, which meant control of the stretch of African coast directly opposite Gibraltar. This was designed to take advantage of French attention being focused elsewhere and as a prelude to an African empire. Though much of this was wishful thinking by Franco, in those heady days of June 1940, when France was at its weakest, German total victory in Europe seemed certain and the collapse of both British and French empires apparently imminent, he could dare to dream. Although Hitler had welcomed Spain's change to non-belligerent, he had no wish for them to go further. Although aware of this, Franco made an offer to join the war on Germany's side in return for France's North African colonies and German support to take Gibraltar and defend the Canary Islands. Hitler declined. Franco's goodwill was assured but other than that, Spain could offer little and relations with the defeated French were more important.

WWII - Churchill Bribes Franco's Generals

At the end of June, Franco dismissed General Yague as Air Minister for involvement in a pro-German coup against the Spanish leader. This highlighted that there were factions within Franco's regime, with a variety of shades of opinion on the level of support that Spain should give to Germany. This was to be exploited by Churchill, with the help of Hoare and an old acquaintance, Alan Hillgarth (see Chapter 4). Together and with the help of others, Churchill and the British Government directly bribed individuals within the upper echelons of the Franco regime, to keep Spain out of the Second World War. A sum of £10 million (worth around £690,000,000 in 2023) "was secretly arranged for selected Spanish Generals from British public funds."[5]

The bribing of Franco's Generals was carried out by Hillgarth, working for British Intelligence in his official position as Naval attaché at the British embassy in Madrid. He arranged this through the auspices of the Mallorcan banker Juan March (see Chapter 4). Churchill met with Hillgarth at length at the end of May and it was then that the plans were laid to transfer enormous sums of money to Franco's cronies to try keep Spain out of the war. The fear by the autumn of 1940 was that Hitler would move forces through Spain (with or without Franco's approval) to capture Gibraltar and not only deny Britain the safe anchorage there, but also effectively control guns on both sides of the Straits. Churchill had lunch with Franco's representative in Britain, his "cousin" the Duke of Alba (see Chapter 8) in December and gave rather abject defence for his vacillating attitude towards the Spanish Civil War. He stated that he had been on the Nationalist side at the beginning and only shifted once Germany and Italy were involved out of his sense of English patriotism. He said he later retracted the statement (given at the

---

5 Richard Wigg, *Churchill and Spain. The survival of the Franco Regime 1940 – 1945*, p 11.

end of 1938) that it would be better if the Nationalists lost. Of course, Churchill said all of this in the hope that it would get back to Franco and he further reassured the Duke that it was his personal intervention which saw Spain provided with food over the last few months.[6]

It was Hitler, rather than anything Franco or his Generals did, which decided the outcome of Spain's intervention. He also decided against moving through Spain to take Gibraltar in the autumn of 1940. By this time planning was well underway for 'Operation Barbarossa' which Germany attack the Soviet Union in June 1941. This was not known to Britain at the time and at the start of 1941 the fear was still very much that Hitler would move into Spain. February of that year saw the death in exile of Alfonso XIII. This produced a nostalgic upsurge in support for the monarchy in Spain, centred around Alfonso's son, Don Juan. Churchill, who had eulogised about Alfonso long before his death and who favoured constitutional monarchy as a system of government, was nonetheless cool in promoting any regime change in Spain. Ambassador Hoare was more forthcoming, "Don Juan is an excellent young man. If I were in his place, I would force the pace."[7] Hoare could have expected a Spain ruled by Don Juan to be more sympathetic to Britain. Don Juan had served in the British Royal Navy and lived in Rome and then Switzerland with his British mother.

Hillgarth made a trip back to Britain in January 1941, where he briefed the Prime Minister, with Churchill stating that he had "long and excellent talks" with Hillgarth. The Naval attaché was then invited to a Cabinet meeting to brief the members there. Churchill had disagreed with the Americans over support to Spain. The view of the US was that Spain should not be supplied with food aid as they were a fascist power. This

---

6 *Ibid.* pp 26-27.
7 Templewood Papers XIII – 16 Correspondence with PM 7.3.41

had been fudged by them in 1940, when, facing a humanitarian disaster in Spain, they had channelled food aid via the Red Cross. There was an argument to say that Britain and the US should not provide food, which would then bring the situation in Spain to a head. Regime change may well move Spain away from the Axis powers, but this was not completely predictable. In any case, Churchill was not interested in regime change and would rather Spain be reliant on Britain and the US so that they would not allow Germany free passage through the country.

Churchill had appointed Eden foreign secretary just before the end of 1940 and in February of the following year he went to Gibraltar to discuss plans to resist should German troops come through Spain. Plans were made to encourage and support Spanish resistance if the Germans entered into Spain uninvited. The bribery scheme appeared to be working when there was a change near the very top of the Spanish regime, when Franco replaced his brother in law, Serrano Suñer, as Interior minister. Suñer retained his foreign minister brief but is was a clear statement by Franco that he was in charge and no one would be allowed to challenge him from within. Hillgarth was delighted as Suñer was very close to the Germans and his replacement could be 'influenced'. The Falange were less pleased, but Franco also reorganised their senior leadership to again display who controlled Spain. On the whole, the Heads of the army were pro-neutrality and considered that it would be potentially very damaging for Spain to join the war; whereas the Falange were very keen on formalising the links between Spain and Germany and Italy. It was therefore the Generals (or at least a selected number of them) that Britain tried to strengthen the hand of, through bribes and other diplomatic channels.

Events took another twist at the end of June 1941, when Germany invaded the Soviet Union. This had an almost immediate effect in Spain. Suñer took advantage by whipping up the Falange to a show of support for Hitler who was taking the fight against Bolshevism directly to Stalin. Franco too openly supported the Nazis as they fought against the "Godless" Soviets, and he approved of the formation of the Blue Division (see Chapter 16). Franco went further in July. In a speech to commemorate the rising, the Spanish dictator harangued Britain and the US. He complained about countries taking advantage of Spain's distress, meaning Britain and America's supply of food and petrol to Spain, in return for them keeping out of the war. This was breathtaking arrogance and lack of humility. Franco was complaining that Britain, locked in a life-or-death struggle for its very existence, was diverting precious resources in order to keep Spaniards from starving. A side effect of this of course was to keep Franco in power by preventing civil unrest.

The brazenness of the speech was not lost on the British. Hillgarth was convinced that Franco had gone too far in aligning himself with the German cause. This would in turn, he believed, lead to those at the top of the army overthrowing the current leadership and establishing a junta to rule Spain. This was a gross exaggeration of the position at the time, although one that Hillgarth genuinely believed. One of the problems with paying people is that they constantly want to appear relevant and on your side in order to keep getting the money. Hillgarth was being duped by Generals who were overplaying their own importance and the pace of change. Eden suspected as much and never thought that any major change in Spain was as close as Hillgarth did.

Franco, as usual, was adept at playing both sides against each other. To the Generals (on the British payroll) who wanted Serrano Suñer replaced as foreign minister for aligning Spain too closely with Germany, Franco said be patient, lest any hint of instability within Spain was to hasten German entry into the country. Publicly, he backed the Germans and was full of praise for the might of their military, but he would go no further than words until there was absolutely no doubt about Nazi victory. Although the Germans were still advancing through Russia as summer came to an end, the campaign had not been as swift as Franco might have desired. A Rommel takeover of the Suez Canal however would signal the end of the British Empire's effectiveness, especially in the Mediterranean region.

Churchill was left frustrated by Hillgarth's flawed reading of the state of readiness of the Spanish Generals to wrest decision making power from Franco. Eden's judgement, that the bribed Generals were overstating their preparedness and their willingness to act, seemed wiser. It may be though that Hillgarth was a little unfortunate as the main reason that General Aranda and others did not establish a ruling Junta was fear of provoking a German invasion. Churchill did intervene with President Roosevelt however when an American ban on movement of cash held in foreign banks in America threatened the Generals' money. The Prime Minister was able to get a secret exemption for the bribed Generals.

In December 1941, the Japanese attacked Pearl Harbour and Germany declared war on America, bringing them into the conflict. Britain suffered severe naval loses to Japan and before the end of the year, the fall of Hong Kong. Italian mines had also severely damaged their capabilities in the Mediterranean and a likely move through Spain seemed even more likely, to take advantage of Britain's weakened position, especially after the blow of the loss of Singapore in February 1942.

In Churchill's account of the Second World War, written in the years immediately afterwards, Churchill praised Franco as if he had been a staunch ally in 1942 as the British and Americans prepared for Operation Torch:

"Spain still held the key to all British enterprises in the Mediterranean and never in the darkest hours did she turn the lock against us."⁸

This was far from being true in 1942 when these events took place. As the Allies prepared for Torch (mass troop landings in Vichy run North Africa), the Germans had been allowed to build watch stations on Spain's southern coast to monitor Allied ship movements. Hoare saw Franco in person to protest at these, saying that they had been built using fuel from Britain and America, a thinly veiled threat to future supplies. Franco was concerned enough to order the posts to be removed.

There were differences in the attitude of Britain and the United States towards Spain over the supply of oil/petrol. In November 1941, just prior to their entry into the war, The Americans had suspended supplies to Spain after it was discovered that the Spanish had been lying to the British about their needs and that Franco had stockpiled fuel. America had called the bluff of Churchill's appeasement of Spain. In truth, Spain was actively resupplying German submarines in the Atlantic using their Atlantic coast and the Canary Islands.

There was much monarchist plotting among some of the generals and others during 1942. Without more definite backing from Britain, they were too scared to act and most thought that they needed the precipitous incursion into Spain of Germany. The "pretender" to the throne, Don Juan, was asked by the British to wait until the war was over before making a move. On 1st September, Franco surprised everyone by sacking Serrano as Foreign Minister. Fighting between royalists and Falange on the streets had seen Franco assert his authority by removing people of both persuasions from top jobs and replacing them with others more likely to blandly follow Franco's lead. Franco was advised that removing Serrano Suñer as well would show that there was nothing personal in his reshuffle. Franco was

---

8 Winston Churchill, *The Second World War Volume IV: The Hinge of Fate*, London, Cassell (1951) p 460.

disposed to this because Suñer was flaunting another mistress, much to the distress of Franco's wife and her sister (Serrano's wife). Franco later claimed that he knew that Operation Torch was being prepared and he removed his pro-German Foreign Minister to assist the Allies, but this was not true.

As the build-up in Gibraltar ahead of Torch became obvious, it was necessary to reassure Franco that Spain was not the intended target, without telling him what the allies were doing. Both Roosevelt, in a personal letter, and Hoare in person, gave assurances about respecting Spain's territorial integrity, on the peninsula and in her colonies. Negotiations around a large consignment of goods for Spain were carefully timed to be at a critical stage when Torch happened, to help focus Franco's mind as he gauged any response. In the end, the Spanish were just glad that it was not them who were the targets, whether on the Spanish mainland or in Morocco. Instead, Britain and American troops made large scale amphibious landings on France's North African coast, from Casablanca to Algiers, on either side of the Straits of Gibraltar. Torch was an almost immediate success and a show of Allied strength close to Spain that Franco could not fail to notice.

16
FRANCO AND HITLER

The relationship between the two dictators was a curious one. They met only once, in a railway carriage in Hendaye in the South of France in October 1940. The meeting had been well planned. Heinrich Himmler had enjoyed a three-day visit to Spain to discuss the arrangements a few days earlier. He enjoyed the full ceremony that Spain could muster, including an arrival parade in Madrid down streets lined with swastikas. Privately he was appalled at the continued repression of Republicans by Franco's regime, with prisons still overflowing and executions continuing unabated. It gives some idea of the scale of the repression in Spain under Franco that the Nazis were shocked at the scale and brutality.

Prior to the meeting, Hitler and Franco had exchanged letters and Suñer had met directly with Hitler. He had assured the Fuhrer of Spain's intention to join the war as soon as foodstuffs and other conditions were correct. Hitler wanted Spain to give him one of the Canary Islands and some other minor overseas territories for his use. Franco wanted French Morocco. Hitler was worried that if this was agreed, even as a war aim rather than for immediate action, then word would leak out. The result of this could be to turn the Vichy French in North Africa against the Axis powers. Until now, especially since the attack on the French fleet by the British at Mers El Kebir in July 1940, the French there had shown no signs of joining the with the Allied powers and indeed Vichy forces had repulsed a raid on French Morocco by the British and free French forces. Any agreement between Hitler and Franco to give French Morocco to Spain would upset the delicate relationship that existed between the Germans and

Vichy France.

The meeting was later portrayed by Franco's apologists as the time when Franco cleverly kept Spain from joining Nazi Germany in the war. This version was only put forward when Franco had to swiftly backpedal as the Allied powers looked like being victorious towards the end of the war and in the immediate wake of their 1945 triumph. The reality in the autumn of 1940 was very different. Franco had already stated to Hitler that he would join on the Axis side when Spain was capable and the meeting in Hendaye was to agree the terms. In the end, the price that Spain wanted for joining was too much for Germany to agree to. The Nazi relationship with Vichy France was more important than the strategic and material advantage that Spain could bring. Hitler was advised by his top aides not to let Spain join the war, "Spain's domestic situation is so rotten as to make her useless as a political partner."[1] They also believed that agreeing to Franco's idea of a share of the spoils (Spain taking over French Morocco) would simply invite the British to attack it.

There are varying accounts of the meeting itself, but they are contradictory. There is one, from a Spanish point of view, which depicts Franco as skilfully resisting Hitler's pressure, with the Fuhrer demanding Spain join him and the Caudillo masterfully deflecting. This was an account which only came to light later, in a post second world war world with a changed landscape. If, at the time, as the account claimed, Hitler had offered Franco Oran (a major city in French Morocco), Franco would have jumped at the chance. More accurate is the account given by the then Spanish Foreign Minister, Serrano Suñer, just a few weeks later, that "there had been no pressure… on the part of Hitler or Mussolini that Spain should join the war."[2] Hitler was more concerned with getting the cooperation of the French (he

---
1 Halder Diary 11/10/40 p262
2 FRUS 1940 II p824

had met Laval the day before and was meeting Pétain the day after) and so would not have promised any of their territories to Spain.

The meeting ended with a dinner and – for Franco – an emotional goodbye in which he pledged to come to Germany's aid if ever this was needed, with no preconditions. Formally an agreement was reached in which Spain agreed to join the Axis powers in the war when Germany required it. Despite all of Franco's later assertions to the contrary, here was a signed agreement to enter the war, at an unspecified later date, on the side of Germany and Italy.

It is fair to say that Hitler had not enjoyed his meeting with Franco and was not keen to repeat it, "rather than go through that again, I would prefer to have three or four teeth taken out,"[3] as he told Mussolini.

Franco had first had contact with Hitler in the immediate aftermath of the attempted coup in July 1936. In Morocco, his contact with local Nazis who had good connections in Germany which could go all the way to Hitler, set him above Mola, who was making modest requests from mainland Spain. The other factor which meant that Franco was successful in his pleas to Hitler for assistance was that he was the head of the Army of Africa, the best part of the Spanish armed forces. Hitler received Franco's request on the evening of 25th and immediately agreed. Franco was delighted and telegrammed Mola on the 29th of July to tell him that "Today the first transport aircraft arrives. We have the upper hand."[4]

Franco's relationship with Hitler throughout the Spanish Civil War was paradoxical. On the one hand they were brothers-in-arms, both fighting against the great evil of communism,

---

3 Ciano papers p402
4 Bande del alzamiento a la guerra civil verano 1936 correspondencia Franco Mola Historia y vida no. 93 (1975), p 21.

albeit Hitler was doing so from a position of relative strength. Franco relied on Germany's (and Italy's) military aid; however, Franco was also proud and independent. Hitler though Franco, slow and plodding and much preferred General Mola in a purely military sense and yet he recognised that Franco had emerged as leader of the Nationalists and that it was through him that German aid would have to be channelled, even though doing so helped secure Franco's leadership position.

Having secured his position of leader of the Nationalists forces, Franco's ambitions grew. By early 1937, Franco was imagining himself as a saviour of the nation, in the manner of Hitler and Mussolini. Indeed, it was at the suggestion of a leading Italian fascist that Franco began to contemplate creating a national political movement which he would control. This would have several advantages for Franco's ambitions. Firstly, Franco did not want it to be either the Falange or the Carlists, the two most powerful political groups on the Nationalist side. By creating something new, Franco could overcome (in theory at least) the bitter rivalries that existed between the two groups. Secondly, he would also be weakening both groups as they would now be subsumed into the new organisation. This would mean that the leaders of the Falange and the Carlists would lose some of their importance and status, making them less of a threat or potential rival to Franco. Thirdly, this move would lend a veneer of political legitimacy to Franco. Until this point, Franco has merely been head of the Nationalist armies. This was Franco looking ahead to the future of Spain once the Nationalists had won. Although he welcomed this Italian suggestion of a new political movement, he rebuffed their other idea at the time of naming the monarchical successor who would take over the throne of Spain once the Civil War was over. Franco was metamorphosising from a *Generalisimo* into a *Cuadillo*.

Prior to the fall of France, Franco's ambassador to

France held a number of meetings with Laval and Pétain, two of France's leading right-wing politicians. The French were trying to establish favourable negotiating terms for future talks with Germany. They discussed strategy with the Spanish ambassador, using him as a sounding board and hoping to be able to count on Spanish support in the new order that would be created after French capitulation. The Spanish ambassador, Lequerica, was under orders from Franco to encourage this and to report the conversations back. He duly did so and Franco sent the reports to the Germans, providing valuable insight into French thinking prior to the agreement that set up the Vichy controlled area.

At the beginning of November 1940, Franco again wrote to Hitler (and Mussolini) pledging his support and willingness to join the war but again staking his claim to North African expansion. At the same time, Spain took control of the city of Tangier, which had been ruled by international administration, incorporating the city into Spanish Morocco. Hitler was encouraged by Franco's letter as it left no doubt as to whose side Spain was on. He now made plans for Spain's entry into the war and the capture of Gibraltar. Suñer was invited to Germany in mid-November for discussions. However, in the two weeks since writing the letter, Franco had had a severe reality check from the heads of the army, navy and air force. They stated that Spain's military was in no fit state to enter a war against the British. Further, Franco was advised, while the British held Suez, the economic results of being at war with Britain and the blockade which would follow, coupled with the ending of British and US aid, would cripple Spain quickly.

Hitler had his staff draw up plans for German troops to enter Spain (with Spanish cooperation) in January 1941 prior to them attacking Gibraltar in February. However, the lack of compatibility of the French and Spanish railways (they were different gauges) and the perilous state of the latter, meant that moving men and equipment south through Spain would not be easy. Franco was also forced to backtrack on his promise to enter the war quickly when he admitted that the food crisis was even worse than previously admitted. Spain was reliant on US aid to prevent many in the country starving over the winter. Franco was also worried that if Spain entered the war, the British would almost immediately take the Canary Islands, as they had plans to do so (see Chapter 17). Franco could not join the war, however much he wanted to. There was never a question of Germany taking Gibraltar by moving troops through Spain against the wishes of the Spanish. This would have inevitably led to further delay to their plans for expansion in the East, already delayed by having to sort out the mess Mussolini had made of the invasion of Greece.

The negotiations between Spain and Germany to bring Spain into the war immediately and therefore permit German troops into Spain to take Gibraltar, came in December 1940. Hitler sent Admiral Canaris, the Head of German Military Intelligence, the *Abwerh*. Canaris was anti-communist and had helped supply the Nationalists directly with weapons (made in Britain) during the Spanish Civil War. However, he was against Germany's military adventurism however and had opposed the invasions of Czechoslovakia and Poland. Canaris had met in secret with British intelligence and was plotting against Hitler throughout most of World War Two. It was therefore unfortunate for Hitler that this was the person he trusted to negotiate Spain's entry into the war. Hitler wanted to send his forces in early in January of 1941, determined that they would be able to move south and take Gibraltar before the start of Operation Barbarossa and the invasion of the Soviet Union, scheduled for Spring. Canaris was not successful – if indeed he ever tried – to get Franco to agree to join the war immediately and thereby permit German troops through Spain. The reality was though that famine and near economic collapse meant that Franco could not afford to join the war. Especially with Britain still in control of Suez, Franco could not risk it.

Hitler had another try at getting Franco to agree to enter the war and therefore allowing German troops to enter Spain and take Gibraltar in January 1941. Although Franco again stated that Spain would join the Axis powers, he would not agree to a timetable which stated that Spain's entry into the war would be when Germany deemed it best. Hitler was not pleased by Franco and made it known that he believed Spain's leader was, "only an average officer, who, because of the accident of circumstance, had been pushed into the position of Head of State. He was not a sovereign but a subaltern in temperament".[5]

Germany's invasion of the Soviet Union in June 1941 brought an opportunity for Franco to slightly redeem himself in the eyes of his fellow dictators. While Franco was worried about involving himself in a war against Britain, with the threat to Spanish territory and trade routes that this entailed, he had no qualms about facing the Soviet Union, albeit at a distance. Spain would not declare war on the Soviet Union however as doing do would have brought them into the war against Britain as well. Franco and Suñer however agreed that volunteers could go from Spain to serve on Hitler's Eastern front. These volunteers would come from the ranks of the Falange and the army and became known as the Blue Division.

Organised by the Spanish army and welcomed by Germany, the Spaniards enlisted in the German army but fought together as a Division. Over 18 000 strong, the soldiers were dressed in a new uniform (they could not use the Spanish army one) which consisted of a red beret to incorporate the Carlists and a blue shirt, hence their name. However, this was largely for show while in Spain. In the field, the troops wore the German

---

5 Quoted in Paul Preston, *Franco*, p 416.

army uniform, with a Spanish emblem on the sleeve. Airmen among the volunteers formed a "blue squadron" and flew German aircraft.

The Blue Division was dispatched to the front by the end of August, joining the Army of the North and taking part, a year later in the siege of Leningrad. Attempts to break the siege by the Soviets saw the Spanish suffer heavy casualties over the next two years. Near the end of 1944, with Franco realising that he did not want to have soldiers still fighting for Germany when they lost the war, the troops were ordered to return to Spain. Some of the soldiers defied this and stayed behind to continue fighting for Germany in what became the "Blue Legion".

In total, almost 50 000 fought in the Blue Division throughout the war, as fresh volunteers replaced those injured or on leave. Around 10% lost their lives with almost 9000 wounded. In terms of their effectiveness, the Blue Division are regarded as having fought very well. They were resolute in defence when maintaining the siege of Leningrad in the face of attacks by Soviet troops who outnumbered the Spaniards. Hitler recognised this by awarding the soldiers a special medal and stated that "the Spaniards have never yielded an inch of ground, one can't imagine more fearless fellows."[6] Speaking in July 1941, Franco could not hide his delight at the prospect of Spanish troops fighting alongside the Germans, even if he was in no position to formally declare war, " The Allies are on the wrong side in this war and they have lost it….the blood of our youth is to mingle with that of our comrades of the Axis as a living expression of our solidarity".[7]

The speech had consequences. There was no longer any doubt, in the eyes of the British and others, that the push within

---

6 Hitler's *Table Talk*.
7 *Bulletin of Spanish Studies*, Volume XVIII No. 72, October 1941, pp 210-217.

Spain to join the war on the side of the Allies did not just come from Suñer and the hard core Falangists, but from Franco himself. Days later the British Cabinet decided to go ahead with plans to take the Canary Islands (see Chapter 17). The British Foreign Secretary, Eden, had long been wary of backing Franco and now considered supporting the Spanish Left in regime change. The Americans responded by cutting the supply of food and oil to Spain until there was virtually none reaching there via America. It was Churchill who pulled back from taking the Canaries and who eventually persuaded the Americans to let some supplies through to Spain (see Chapter 15). At the end of November 1941, America sent Spain the terms on which it was willing to continue trading with them, which were being considered by Franco when the Japanese bombed Pearl Harbor on 7th December. Franco sent the Japanese a telegram of congratulations. Spanish glee was quickly tempered by the Japanese invasion of the Philippines, a former Spanish colony and the subsequent entry into the war of a number of Latin American countries on the side of the Allies.

From the bombastic imperial demands as his price of entry in the summer of 1940, to his more sober assessment of the harsh realities of life in Spain under his rule in winter and early 1941, Franco's position on joining the Axis powers was always pragmatic, regardless of how strongly he desired it. The German invasion of the Soviet Union had provided a chance for Franco's military to perform on the world stage, albeit at arm's length; and Franco's speech in July had demonstrated his true feelings, untrammelled due to his absolute belief in Axis victory. The entry into the war of the USA and the Japanese expansion to the South and East further complicated matters, but there was never any doubt where Franco's loyalties lay. During 1942, Franco watched and waited but by the end of that year it was plain to see that the tide was turning in favour of the Allies. He would need all his self-preservation skills to see out the war and its aftermath intact. That he would do so was not down to his links with Hitler or other Axis leaders but to the intervention of Churchill.

17
GIBRALTAR, OPERATION PILGRIM AND OPERATION MINCEMEAT

It should be clear from the preceding chapter that Gibraltar played a significant role in relations between Britain and Spain during World War Two, both due to the strategic importance of its position and in the toing and froing that saw Germany trying to persuade Spain to enter the war. Gibraltar had also been an important consideration during the Spanish Civil War. It had certainly been part of the consideration of Mussolini in deciding to assist Franco. A friendly fellow dictator in charge of Gibraltar could control entry to the Mediterranean and thereby assist Italy in ousting Britain as the dominant naval power in the area – Spain's navy being unlikely to be a serious rival to Italy.

As German and Italian planes flew over the Straits of Gibraltar to transport the Army of Africa at the outbreak of the Spanish Civil War, they were spotted by the British stationed there. This was not publicised widely however, even though it was indisputable early proof of the involvement of those countries. This was due to the sympathies of the British in Gibraltar who were decidedly in favour of the Nationalists and deliberately aided them at times. The officers in charge had been appalled when the Spanish ratings had overthrown their officers during the attempted rising of the Generals and saved the ships for the Republic. An objective view may have judged this to be loyal sailors quashing a traitorous act by the officers. To the class obsessed senior service officers of the Royal Navy, it was tantamount to revolution. The Invergordon mutiny was fresh in their minds and they, more than any other part of the British armed forces or government, directly aided the Nationalists throughout the war. Early in the Spanish conflict, the Germans in Spain were reporting back that the British in Gibraltar had been supplying weapons to the Nationalists and that "the British Cruiser commander here (in Gibraltar) has recently been supplying us with information on Russian arms deliveries to the red government, which he certainly would not do without instruction".[1]

This implies that the attitude – and actions – of the commanders in Gibraltar in helping the Nationalists were officially sanctioned. In the early days of the war, before the policy of non-intervention, this is probably true. That the officers in Gibraltar would push their orders in favour of the Nationalists to the limits is not in dispute, however it is unlikely that they would have acted in contradiction of any direction to retain strict neutrality. The actions of those in Gibraltar help to make the case that in the early days of the war, that the British Government were pro-Nationalist. Throughout the Spanish Civil War, those in Gibraltar continued to aid the Nationalists and their friends in less direct but still effective ways. General Kindelan was given facilities to communicate with Berlin and Rome and there was an incident involving the British warship, HMS Queen Elizabeth when the battleship was deliberately moved in front of the port of Algeciras to prevent the Republicans shelling the place. Considering most of the British Government's information about events in Spain came from naval officers, ex naval officers, such as Hillgarth, or from the pro-Nationalist ambassador, Sir Henry Chilton, who refused to stay in Madrid during the war while the capital was controlled by the Republicans and spent his

---

1 German Charge di affairs, Hans Voelckers, quoted in Antony Beevor, *The Battle for Spain*, p 73.

Gilbraltar, Operation Pilgrim and Operation Mincemeat

time in France.[2] This Gibraltar/naval influence was crucial to the formation of British Government policy towards the Civil War and also in confirming Churchill's natural inclinations towards the conflict at its outbreak and for some time afterwards.

During the second World War, Gibraltar played a crucial part in the thinking of Churchill and Hitler in shaping their stance towards Spain and the possibility of direct involvement in the war (see Chapter 16). Its strategic position would not be given up cheaply by the British and was coveted by the Axis powers. Operation Torch underlined Gibraltar's importance to the Allies and the North African invasion would have been extremely difficult if not impossible without having control of Gibraltar. Hitler promised that if Franco allowed German troops through Spain to take Gibraltar, then the Rock would be returned to Spain at the end of the war. In the mind of the German leader, Gibraltar was the main reason that he wanted Spain to join the Axis powers.

Gibraltar was also the host of a British SOE section, aimed at disrupting Spain through economic warfare and sabotage should Franco be tempted to join the Axis powers. The group was never utilised, although clandestine operations, many of which were to prevent Spanish export of Wolfram to Germany did take place, largely under the direction of Hillgarth. The British outpost in the South of the Iberian Peninsula had played a small but partisan role in the Spanish Civil War; in World War Two, Gibraltar was pivotal in the intrigues that surrounded the possibility of Spanish entry to the war and often the only real factor. A note sent by Churchill to President Roosevelt at the beginning of 1942, a month after the US had been brought

---

2 Sir Henry did not even stay in Hendaye in the South of France for too long, taking an extended period of leave before resigning as ambassador prior to the end of 1937. He vehemently supported the Nationalists and only returned to Madrid in 1939 to collect his belongings, once Franco was in charge.

into the war, shows its strategic importance and the connection between Gibraltar and the means by which Spain was being kept out of the war:

"Please will you very kindly consider giving a few rationed carrots to the Dons to starve off trouble at Gibraltar? Every day we have use of the harbour is a gain."[3]

In retaliation for any Spanish entry to World War Two – and the likely seizure of Gibraltar which would shortly follow – Churchill planned a British takeover of the Canary Islands, called Operation Pilgrim. This was a reaction to the proposed Operation Felix, which Hitler abandoned in 1941 after Franco's dithering over entering the war. However, plans to occupy the Canary Islands had begun before this.

At the start of World War Two, the Germans had been concerned that the Spanish may not defend the islands in the event of a British occupation. They also believed that the Canaries, Cape Verdes, Maderia and the Azores (the last two being Portuguese) were vulnerable to British takeover and were also of strategic importance to trade routes. Part of Operation Felix, the German plan to go through Spain to take Gibraltar included a pre-emptive occupation of the Azores. Convinced, since the meeting between Franco and Hitler at Hendaye, that the Spanish would resist any British attempt to take the Canaries, another element of the proposed German operation was to reinforce the Canary Islands' defences. Plans were also put in place to bolster the meagre defences of the Cape Verde islands. It was clear to the Germans by February of 1941 that Franco's prevaricating over entry to the war was not going to be overcome. Operation Felix was cancelled, although defensive reinforcement of the Canary Islands did take place later that year and continued for some time.

The British were concerned that the Germans would use

---

3 David Stafford, *Roosevelt and Churchill*, p 313.

the Azores or the Canaries as a U-boat base, but it was the threat of losing Gibraltar which was the basis of Operation Pilgrim. Churchill stated that, "If we are forced from Gibraltar, we must take the Canaries immediately, allowing us to control the western entry to the Mediterranean".[4] This was the prompt for Operation Pilgrim.

Operation Pilgrim was the name given to the amalgamation of the planning of three invasions: Azores (Operation Thruster), Maderia (Operation Springboard) and the Canaries and Cape Verde (Operation Puma). Pilgrim became focused more on the Canary Islands as these were seen as the most important strategically and the best defended, therefore in need of the most careful planning. The specific objective was to take Gran Canaria and a formidable force was being assembled to accomplish this. Training in Britain were Canadian troops and SOE totalling 24 000 men. They were to be conveyed to the Canary Islands on board HMS Queen Emma with an invasion fleet consisting of 35 capital ships plus auxiliary support. Two squadrons of RAF fighters would also protect them. The plan was for two Canadian infantry battalions to make an amphibious landing to silence the artillery pieces before a second landing would capture the island's airport. Tenerife would be the next target, with 30 SOE operatives set to parachute in order to conduct clandestine operations which would enable a landing to capture the island.

This was an ambitious plan which would have had a significant impact on the war, either if it was successful (highly likely but never definite) or unsuccessful. The plan to take the Azores was shelved once it became known that if the Germans came into the Iberian Peninsula (with or without Spain's blessing) the Portuguese government planned to relocate to the Azores. On doing this, they would then invite the British or the Americans

---

4 *Gazette Life, Churchill's Canaries*, 28th November 2019.

to protect the islands. Since the trigger for Operation Pilgrim was the same one which would initiate the Portuguese move to the Azores, that part of the plan would never be needed. The main part of the operation, to take the Canary Islands, was put on hold, but troops were held in readiness throughout 1941. As 1942 started it became clear that America's entry into the war and Hitler's failure to beat the Soviets as quickly as he had predicted meant that the Axis victory was not certain. Franco changed Spain's official position back from non-belligerence to neutrality and the threat of German invasion of the Iberian Peninsula was gone. Operation Pilgrim was stood down in February 1942.

In 1943, Spain became the setting of one of the most audacious and successful subterfuge strategies of World War Two. If the true story of Operation Mincemeat sounds like a plot from a James Bond novel, it may be because the idea came originally from one of the suggestions at the beginning of the war for counter espionage from Ian Fleming. With the Allies planning the beginning of the taking back of Europe by invading Sicily, they were nervous of their plans being discovered and the island's defences made ready to repel the attack. Operation Mincemeat planned to deceive the Axis powers into thinking that the invasion was going to be through Greece and Sardinia, with any seeming interest in Sicily merely a ruse.

To accomplish this, British Intelligence would plant false documents on a corpse to be washed up in Spain. The British hoped that the documents would be copied by the Spanish and given to the Germans. The Casablanca conference in January 1943, between Churchill and Roosevelt had agreed that Sicily would be the target of opening up another front by attacking the soft underbelly of the south of Europe. Churchill had prevailed at Casablanca in preventing the US from pushing for an invasion of France in 1943 which he believed would be premature and lead to unacceptable Allied casualties. The main problem with

Sicily was that it was the obvious choice. Something would have to be done to throw the Axis powers off the scent.

A fake Headquarters was set up in Cairo to coordinate a planned invasion of Greece and the Balkans. Dummy tanks, fake manoeuvres for the fictional 12th army and Greece currency and maps were stockpiled, all to throw the Germans off the scent. The real command centre for the actual invasion of Sicily was in Tunis and kept as low a profile as possible by reducing radio messages. The other major piece of deception was to place false documents on a corpse to be washed up in Spain – Operation Mincemeat.

The body of a deceased tramp, later identified as Glyndwr Michael, a Welshman who died from ingesting rat poison, was to be used as the corpse of the fictional Major William Martin of the Royal Marines. The backstory to this fictitious officer was extensive. The corpse was furnished with several documents, including bank and solicitor's correspondence, a letter from his father and even a photograph of a fiancé with love letters. Tickets stubs and receipts were also included, to prove a date that the Major had been in London and show that the 'documents' he was carrying were recent. The documents themselves were carefully thought through. Not only would they name Greece as the location for the invasion and Sicily as the decoy, but they were also in an unofficial letter, as any official correspondence would have been coded or sent in an encrypted signal.

The documents were placed in a briefcase, attached to the tunic of the body with a chain. The corpse was meant to have died following a plane crash, but to transport the body close to the Spanish coast, a submarine was used. Calculations had been made which meant that tides should wash the body up close to Huelva. On 30th of April, 1943, the corpse was released from a submarine off of the Spanish coast. The body was found by a fisherman that morning and handed to the Spanish authorities.

The local British vice-consul, who had been fully informed of the operation, was present at the postmortem which was carried out without any suspicion that the corpse was not as it seemed and the body was buried with full military honours.

The plan worked. The British sent encrypted signals desperately seeking the return of the briefcase, in the full knowledge that the Germans had cracked this code. The briefcase and its contents were transported to Madrid and the German Abwehr were given access to it. The contents of the letters were dried out, copied and then resoaked in sea water before being resealed and handed to the British. Examination showed that the contents had been removed and returned. Bletchley Park intercepted coded German signals showing that they now believed that the Balkans were the target and Hitler was convinced that Greece and Sardinia would be the landing points, based on documents the Germans had obtained.

What the success of the plan showed was that the Spanish could be relied on to aid the Germans and it was this aspect of their Axis bias that the Allies played on. Churchill effectively used Franco to dupe Hitler and it worked.

By 1943, Franco was realising that he had to seriously reposition himself and Spain in order to prevent enforced regime change as the prospect of an Allied victory increased. In the first half of the year, the Battle of the Atlantic reached its peak and the losses to Allied, particularly supplies to Britain were significant. This came against the backdrop of gains for the Allies, especially in North Africa. In July, the fall of Mussolini was a blow to Franco and a reminder that dictators could be toppled. Franco tried to portray himself as a possible go-between who could help negotiate peace between Hitler and the UK/USA. This was never going to be taken seriously. However, 1943 also saw a significant split in policy towards Spain which was to continue and deepen as the second World War drew slowly towards a close.

After the defeat of the Germans in Tunisia, the threat of Spain being occupied by Germany seemed to lessen and the British Chiefs of Staff and the Americans wanted to use this to put more pressure on Franco. There is no doubt that from 1943 onwards, there was less and less reason to keep Franco sweet and yet that it is what Churchill wanted to do. Up until this point, the attitude towards Spain was understandable within the context of the war. The massive amounts of money in bribes and the granting of scarce resources to a country which at best was not a supporter of the Allies and in fact had pledged to join the Axis powers when the time was right, was excusable considering the benefits of not having Franco join Hitler and Mussolini. That it was only the dire state of Spain that meant they didn't join the Axis does not mean that the policy was not needed. It was the combination of the desperate need of Spain and provision by the Allies which kept the country as a non-belligerent. Twice in 1943, British Service Chiefs urged a reconsideration of policy towards Spain and both times Churchill resisted, reassuring the Duke of Alba that Franco had nothing to fear from Britain. This helped Franco resist a plea from his fellow Generals in September 1943 that he should step down in order to prevent the country being treated harshly in the event of (an increasingly likely) Allied victory.

At the end of 1943, The US decided on a unilateral change in policy towards Spain in line with the harder line which being advocated by the army chiefs. Petrol supplies would be halted unless the Spaniards' lucrative trade exporting wolfram[5] to Germany ceased. The British policy had been to try to outbid Germany for the supply of wolfram, which resulted in Franco being able to begin to rebuild Spain's gold reserves as the substance became their most important export. This also

---

5 Wolfram is the ore from which tungsten is produced. Tungsten was used to make armour piercing shells.

marked the beginning of a significant divergence in policy towards Spain between Britain and the US. Even on the British side there were different strands of opinion. For the moment Eden and the foreign office sided with Churchill but this was to change as the war progressed until Churchill was practically the lone voice among the Allies, pleading the cause of Franco.

EPILOGUE: VICTORY IN 1945 AND THE DEFEAT OF THE DICTATORS*
(*EXCEPT IN SPAIN)

The US followed through on their threat in January of 1944 and stopped oil reaching Spain, in order to get them to cease supplying Germany with wolfram. Britain offered to mediate in this dispute, in the hope of currying favour with Spain in future. Roosevelt felt this was Churchill appeasing a dictator. Churchill said that Britain would supply Spain unilaterally in May, in return for a modest cut in the supply of wolfram to Germany. This angered the Americans and had long lasting consequences for British – US relations. Those among the American policy makers who favoured joint, coordinated US-UK foreign policy decisions were sidelined and replaced by others who put American business interests first. Churchill's decision to stick his neck out in order to support Franco not only appeased a dictator but did so for no obvious British gain.

Churchill was looking to the future, to an extent. Of course, he was inclined to support the Duke of Alba and had no overriding objection to Franco's regime, as long as it did not affect British trade. His hope in outflanking the Americans over the oil embargo was that Britain would usurp their allies in trade with the Spanish. Since most of the oil came from America, there was little chance of this once the US restarted supplies. Churchill's support of Franco therefore did not benefit Britain commercially directly. What Churchill did perceive however was the division of the post-war world into spheres of influence. Churchill did not want Spain to be under any obligation to the Soviet Union and would prefer a dictator to a left leaning democracy. He was even prepared to forego his preferred option of monarchy, given that this would necessitate a regime change and the outcome of any upheaval in Spain was uncertain.

To ensure that Franco and anyone considering plotting against him was aware of Churchill's benevolence towards the Spanish dictator, he gave full voice to his Spanish policy in the House of Commons. This was picked up by the American media who were scathing in their criticism of Churchill. Public sentiment in the US was very much against Franco. A little stung by these attacks and anxious to repair the damage he had done to his relationship with Roosevelt, Churchill wrote to the American President in June 1944:

"I see some of your newspapers are upset at my references in the House of Commons to Spain. This is very unfair… I do not care about Franco but I do not wish to have the Iberian peninsula hostile to Britain after the war."[1]

The language which had been used by Churchill in the House of Commons just a few weeks before in May had been unambiguous. Churchill not only gave succour to the Francoist regime during the war but clearly indicated that there would be no change afterwards instigated from outside.

"I look forward to increasingly good relations with Spain… which will, I trust, grow even during the war and will extend after the peace. As I am speaking here today kindly words about Spain, let me add I hope she will be a strong influence for the peace of the Mediterranean after the war. Internal political problems in Spain are a matter for the Spaniards themselves. It is not for us to meddle in such affairs."[2]

---

1 Churchill Archives Cambridge – 120/692 M 731/4 19.6.44
2 *Hansard* 24.5.44

Epilogue: Victory in 1945 and the Defeat of the Dictators

The remarks were disowned by the coalition Labour Party and their damaging nature was recognised by Eden and the Foreign Office. Frantic attempts were made in Spain – where the Franco regime was greatly encouraged by the speech – by ambassador Hoare to readjust the British line and ensure that the Spanish Government were aware that Britain still disliked the Falange and what it stood for.

Towards the end of the year there was evidence of a further split between Churchill and everyone else. By this time, with Paris liberated and the Red Army making progress towards Germany, Churchill was increasingly obsessed with the shape of the post war world. He personally intervened in the civil war in Greece to ensure that the communists did not win and a monarchy was restored. In August he had told the Italians that there were tests for what was acceptable for a country to be considered a democracy:

"Have the people the right to turn out a government of which they disapprove? Is the peasant or workman... free from the fear that some grim police organisation under the control of a single party will tap him on the shoulder and pack him off to bondage or ill treatment."[3]

Although Churchill was clearly warning the Italians of any return to Mussolini's Italy, he could easily have been talking about conditions in Franco's Spain. His actual words on Spain were greatly different.

In October 1944, with the inevitability of an Allied victory now certain and Franco's fear for his own position uppermost in his mind, he tried a personal plea to Churchill to try to save himself. This was made via a letter personally delivered by the Duke of Alba, who still had incredible access to Churchill. In this Franco suggested a post war Anglo-Spanish anti Bolshevik

---

3 Winston Churchill, *The Second World War, Volume VI, Triumph and Tragedy* Message of 28.8.44, p 111,

alliance. While a reply to the letter was being contemplated, another letter arrived, addressed personally to Churchill from General Aranda. This letter had been smuggled from Spain by someone from the British Institute in Madrid. This pleaded with Churchill to increase the pressure on Franco and tighten the economic blockade as the Spanish leader was feeling the pressure. In contrast to Churchill's response to the Duke of Alba, this plea received short shrift and no response was made. The person from the British Institute who had brought it was rebuked.

A response to Franco's Duke of Alba letter was drawn up by the Foreign Office and with Eden's approval, was based on a memorandum by Hoare who was back in London in October 1944. With there no longer being any threat of German invasion of Spain or of the Franco joining Hitler, Hoare was being recalled as ambassador, his special mission was no longer required. He wanted to make it clear that there could be no normal relations between Britain and Spain while the latter retained a system so distant from the United Nations ideal, as outlined by Churchill in Italy. Hoare had also maintained that there must be a joint approach with the Americans, which the Foreign Secretary agreed. Attlee warned that there was a danger that Britain could be seen as the Francoist regime's only supporter, "There is not one of our allies who would not want to see this regime destroyed."[4]

Churchill read the carefully drafted Foreign Office response, which had taken into account the latest dispatches from Madrid, Hoare's memorandum, Attlee's ideas and was calculated to increase the pressure on Franco, ensuring him there would be no easy transition for Spain into the new world order while it was still a totalitarian regime. Churchill wrote an astonishing reply to the Foreign Office and in it, "all his prejudices and ignorance of the Spanish situation are laid bare." Churchill berated Eden,

---

4 War Cabinet Paper (44) 622

Epilogue: Victory in 1945 and the Defeat of the Dictators

believing that starting with oil sanctions would be the thin end of the wedge and would lead to other action which could topple Franco. Churchill stated openly that there was a risk that the Communists could get in if that was the case and if they were in Spain, "we must expect the infection to spread very fast through both Italy and France."[5] Churchill was vitriolic and scathing in attacking Hoare; he said the reply showed left-wing bias in the Foreign Office (of which there had never been any sign and was frankly a preposterous suggestion); he accused Eden of political naivety which would play into the hands of left wing opponents. This was Churchill of old, the war time consensus put aside and the class bias and frothing at Bolshevism to the fore. Churchill also told Eden not to bother the United States with this, confirming the growing belief in the US that Churchill was supporting all of the most reactionary elements in Europe.

Eden was measured in his reply to Churchill and suggested that the Prime Minister reply to Franco's letter himself, hoping that this would be more considered than Churchill's earlier outburst. Although this proved at least partly correct, Churchill could still not be persuaded to include America. This was a major flaw as Franco was adept at playing one faction off against another, indeed it was one of foremost talents. Franco went on to tell the British that the (meagre) threats made of possible consequences were irrelevant as the Spanish could be supplied by America. Without a coordinated approach by the UK and US, Franco could then say something similar to the Americans. This was a direct result of Churchill's actions. He did not give the Americans a copy of Franco's letter for two months.

The reply sent by Churchill was the greatest of the favours he bestowed upon Franco. Due to a mistake in the foreign office, it did not arrive until January of 1945. In his reply, Churchill

---

5 PM's Personal Minutes no. M 1101, 10th November 1944 in FO 371 c 16068, p 124.

crucially omitted the two conditions that Eden had put on Franco's regime being admitted into the international fold post war. The first concerned the internal conditions in Spain, where political executions were still being carried out regularly. Secondly, that the Spanish Government would have to follow the basic tenets of a free and democratic society. Churchill only made reference to Spain not being admitted, thereby taking the pressure off of Franco and allowing the Spanish dictator to portray the attitude of other countries as anti-Spanish rather than anti-Franco. Instead of being seen as excluding itself from the world community by the oppressive nature of its regime and therefore susceptible to challenge from within, Franco rallied support against the rest of the world being anti-Spain and appealed to patriotism. Churchill had not just let Franco off the hook, he had allowed the Spanish dictator to survive. By July 1945, Churchill had been voted out of office. Franco was still the dictator of Spain when he died in 1975.

REFERENCES

WORKS BY CHURCHILL
The Spanish Tragedy (1936)
Keep out of Spain (1936)
A Testing Time for France (1936)
An Object Lesson from Spain (1936)
No Intervention in Spain (1937)
Can the Powers Bring Peace to Spain? (1937)
The Dictators Have Smiled (1937)
Spain's Road to Peace (1937)
Panorama of 1937 (1937)
Great Contemporaries (1937)
Red Sunset in Spain (1938)
Britain and Italy (1938)
Shadows over Czechoslovakia (1938)
The Rape of Austria (1938)
The Spanish Ulcer (1938)
Hope in Spain (1939)
After President Roosevelt's Message (1939)
Step by Step 1936-1939 (1939)
The Second World War Volume I: The Gathering Storm (1948)
The Second World War Volume IV: The Hinge of Fate (1951)

WORKS ABOUT CHURCHILL
Martin Gilbert, *Winston S. Churchill: The Coming of War 1922-1939* (1976)
Roy Jenkins, *Churchill* (2001)
Leo McKinstry, *Attlee and Churchill: Allies in War, Adversaries in Peace* (2019)

Clive Ponting, *Churchill* (1994)
David Reynolds, *In Command of History: Churchill Fighting and Writing the Second World War* (2004)
Robert Rhodes James, *Winston S. Churchill: His Complete Speeches* (1974)
Andrew Roberts, *Churchill* (2018)
David Stafford, *Roosevelt and Churchill Men of Secrets* (1999)
Anthony Tucker-Jones, *Churchill Master and Commander: Winston Churchill at War 1895 - 1945* (2021)
Richard Wigg, *Churchill and Spain. The survival of the Franco Regime 1940–1945* (2008)

WORKS ABOUT FRANCO/SPAIN
Rogelio Baon, *La cara humana de un caudillo* (1975)
Antony Beevor, *The Battle for Spain: The Spanish Civil War 1936-1939* (2006)
Peter Day, *Franco's Friends* (2011)
Gazette Life (magazine), *Churchill's Canaries*, 28th November 2019
Willy Maley (Ed.), *Our Fathers Fought Franco* (2023)
George Orwell, *Homage to Catalonia* (1938)
Paul Preston, *A Concise History of the Spanish Civil War* (1996)
Paul Preston, *The Spanish Civil War, Reaction, Revolution and Revenge* (2006)
Paul Preston, *Franco* (1993)
Paul Preston, *The Spanish Holocaust* (2012)
Giles Tremlett, *The International Brigades* (2020)
Eugenio Vegas Latapie, *La frustración en la Victoria: memorias politicas* (1995)
Richard Wigg, *Churchill and Spain. The survival of the Franco Regime 1940–1945* (2008)

OTHER - PRIMARY

Manuel Azaña, *Obras completes de Manuel Azaña*, Volume IV (2008)
Galeazzo Ciano Papers National Archives (United States)
Bulletin of Spanish Studies Volume XVIII no 72 October 1941
Churchill Archive Cambridge – 120/692 M 731/4 19.6.44 (1944)
Francisco Franco/ Emilio Mola Bande Del alzamiento a la Guerra civil Verano de 1936: correspondencia FrancoMolaHistoria y vida no 93 (1975)
Foreign Relations of the United States Volume II (1940)
Franz Halder, T*he Halder Diaries: The Private War Journals of Colonel General Franz Halder* (1976)
Hermann Goering at the Nuremberg trials in Paul Preston, *The Spanish Civil War, Reaction, Revolution and Revenge* p153-154
Hansard (various)
Hitler's TableTalk, The Complete Edition 1941-1944 (2023)
Dolores Ibárruri, "Farewell address" Speech, Barcelona, Spain
Mussolini to Franco 9 June 1940, *Documenti Diplomatici Italiana serie 9*, volume IV, p620 (Rome 1960)
The National Archives: FO371/2025W7476
PM's Personal Minutes no. M 1101, 10th November 1944 in FO 371 c 16068 p124
Templewood Papers XIII – 16 Correspondence with PM 7.3.41
La Vanguardia (newspaper) 13 December 1935
War Cabinet papers 1944

OTHER - SECONDARY

Anthony Beevor, *Revolution and Civil War 1917 – 1921*
Jimmy Burns, *Papa Spy* (2009)
Peter Duff Hart-Davis, *Man of War* (2012)
Keith Middlemass and John Barnes, *Baldwin, A Biography* (1969)

INDEX

Abyssinia 38, 47, 48, 54, 63, 75, 83, 84, 118
AC (Acció Catalana) 58
Alba, Duke of 77, 89, 97, 98, 108, 169, 195, 197, 199, 200
Alcalá-Zamora, Niceto 27, 29, 33-35, 43-45, 52, 53, 56, 58, 64, 71
Alfonso XIII 8-10, 16, 17, 21, 25-28, 39, 41, 42, 170
Army of Africa 16, 46, 65, 66, 70, 72, 75, 76, 82, 90, 101, 102, 106, 111, 117, 143, 146, 147, 151, 179, 187
Astray, Millán 16
Attlee, Clement Richerd 33, 47, 157, 165, 200
Aranda, Antonio (General) 173, 200
Azaña Diaz, Manuel 29, 33-35, 39-41, 43, 44, 51, 57, 58, 60, 64, 65, 72, 73, 80, 85
Aznar-Cabañas, Juan Bautista (Admiral) 26, 27

Baldwin, Stanley 19, 21, 23, 30, 47-50, 62, 63, 82, 83, 104, 117
Barrio, Diego Martínez 58, 72, 73
Bebb, Cecil 69-71, 82, 86
Berenguer y Fusté, Dámasco (General) 21, 26, 27
Besteiro, Julián 159
Blum, Léon 102, 103, 105
Bolin, Luis 68, 69, 70, 101

Calvo Sotelo, Jose 20, 67-69, 86, 117
Carlists 55, 59, 65, 71, 96, 97, 180, 183
Casares Quiroga, Santiago 64, 71, 72
CEDA (Confederación Española de Derechas Autónomas) 43-46, 52, 54, 55, 57, 59, 60, 91, 95, 100
Chamberlain, Neville 49, 51, 63, 98, 105, 152, 155-157, 165
Chilton, Sir Henry 188
Churchill, Winston
and:
   Alba, Duke of 77, 97, 98, 169, 195, 197, 199, 200
   Alfonso XIII 10, 27,28, 170

Baldwin 19, 2, 23, 30, 48, 49, 63
   being Chancellor 8,19
   being a Conservative MP 9, 19
   being First Lord of the Admiralty 10, 51, 52
   being a Liberal MP 9, 18
Blum, Leon 105
Chamberlain, Neville 49, 51, 63, 105, 157, 165
Czechoslovakia 152, 162
Eden, Anthony 48, 125, 171, 173, 196, 200, 201, 202
Edward VIII 56
father 7
Franco 120, 128, 153, 154, 155
general strike 20
Germany 22, 38, 42, 43, 46, 54, 62 - 64, 78, 79, 84, 101, 105, 114, 119-124, 127, 128, 153-155, 161, 194
Ghandi 32, 33
gold standard 20
Hillgarth, Alan 49 -52, 169-173
Hitler 42, 49, 62, 63, 80, 105, 126-128, 169, 189, 194
India 30, 32, 33, 42, 43
Italy 11, 21, 22, 48, 54, 78, 79, 84, 101, 105, 119-124,126-128, 154, 161, 199-201
Japan 19, 35, 37-39, 127
Largo Caballero, Francisco 106
Mussolini 21,22, 35, 37, 38, 48,54, 78, 80, 84, 126-128, 199
Russian Civil War 13, 14, 80, 81
Soviet Union 39, 74, 80, 81, 102, 105, 198
Spain 78-?, 153-155, 157-159, 161-163
Tonypandy 9,10
Ciano, Galeazzo 101, 168
CNT (Confederación Nacional del Trabajo) 17, 45, 55, 58, 134
Cuba 7
Czechoslovakia 62, 118, 138, 140, 152, 156, 157, 162, 182

Eden, Anthony Robert 48, 82, 83, 98, 103, 104, 123, 125, 155, 156, 170-173, 185, 196,

206

Index

199-202
ERC (Esquerra Republicana de Catalunya) 58

FAI ((Federación Anarquista Ibérica) 55
Falange Española 64, 67, 75, 87, 91, 95-97, 100, 171, 172, 174, 180, 183, 185, 199
Fanjul Goñi, Joaquín (General) 87, 117
France 13, 15, 17, 48, 55, 62, 63, 75, 76, 78, 83, 94, 101-105, 108, 114, 122, 123, 125, 126, 131, 133, 136, 138, 140, 142, 154, 155, 157-161, 163, 166, 168, 175, 177, 178, 180, 181, 189, 192, 201
Franco, Francisco and:
  Army of Africa 16, 17, 45, 65, 66
  Asturias uprising 46, 51, 53, 89
  Azaña 33, 34, 41, 51, 65
  Bebb, Cecil 70, 71, 82
  Bolin, Luis 70
  Calvo Sotelo, Jose 67, 68, 86, 117
  Carlists 96, 180
  Ciano, Galeazzo 168
  Falange 95-97, 171, 172, 174, 180, 185,
  Fanjul Goñi, Joaquín (General) 87, 117
  Franco, Nicolás 89, 91, 92, 96
  Franco, Ramón 25, 89-91
  Germany 70, 91, 96, 97, 101-104, 110, 113-115, 117, 118, 122, 127, 161, 165, 166, 168, 172, 177-185, 189, 192, 194
  Head of military academy 28, 33,34
  Hitler 97, 102, 113-115, 126-128, 166, 170, 172, 177-185, 190, 194, 195, 200
  Italy 70, 91, 102, 109, 117, 118, 167, 168, 179, 180
  Japan 185
  Mola y Vidal, Emilio (General) 64, 65, 66, 75, 87, 95, 96, 101, 113, 117, 120, 179, 180
  Mussolini 70, 9, 101, 109-111, 123, 167, 168, 178-181, 187, 192, 195
  Parents 8
  Puente Bahamonde, Ricardo de la (Major) 89, 90
  Rif War 16
  Sanjurjo/Sanjurjada 40, 41, 66, 86
Franco, Nicolás 89, 91, 92, 96
Franco, Ramón 25, 26, 89-91

Germany 11, 13, 22, 34, 38, 42-44, 46, 48, 54, 58, 61-64, 70, 75, 78-80, 83, 84, 91, 94, 96, 97, 99, 101-105, 109, 110, 113-124, 127-129, 131, 132, 135-137, 139, 141, 145, 149, 152-157, 159, 162, 165-174, 177-185, 187-195, 197, 199, 200
Gibraltar 108, 109, 167, 168-171, 175, 1811183, 187-191
Gil-Robles y Quiñones, José María 44, 45, 52-54, 57, 58, 61, 67, 75, 100
Giral y Pereira, José 33, 73, 80, 102, 138
Goded Llopis, Manuel (General) 87
Goering, Hermann 114
Guernica 116, 117, 127, 155

Hillgarth, Alan 49-52, 54, 169-173, 188, 189
Himmler, Heinrich 177
Hitler, Adolf 42, 44, 49, 61-63, 68, 76, 80, 83, 97, 100, 102, 105, 109, 113-115, 118, 123, 126-128, 140, 152, 156, 157, 162, 165, 166-170, 172, 177-185, 189, 190, 192, 194, 195, 200
Hoare, Samuel, Sir (Viscount Templewood) 48, 83, 166, 167, 169, 170, 174, 175, 199-201

Kun, Bela 80, 81

Ibárruri, Dolores (La Pasionaria) 144, 152
ICE (Izquierda Communista de España) 81
India 30, 32, 42, 43
Italy 11, 14, 17, 21, 22, 37, 38, 47, 48, 54, 63, 70, 75, 78-80, 83,84, 91, 97, 101-105, 109-113, 117-129, 131, 132, 136-139, 141, 148, 149, 151, 152, 154-157, 161, 162, 165-169, 171, 173, 179, 180, 182, 187, 199-201

Japan 13, 19, 34, 35, 37-39, 63, 127, 173, 185
Jerrold, Douglas 68

Lansbury, George 20, 47
Largo Caballero, Francisco 106, 126, 132-134, 142, 161
Lerroux Garcia, Alejandro 31, 44-46, 52, 53, 57, 60

Lloyd George, David 31, 32, 49, 112

MacDonald, Ramsey 18, 23, 30-33, 42, 46, 47
Maley, James 147
March, Juan 51, 52, 59, 68, 169
Maura, Miguel 29
Mexico 68, 136
Mitford, Jessica 94
Mola y Vidal, Emilio (General) 64-67, 70, 71, 72, 75, 86, 87, 95, 96, 101, 102, 113, 117, 120, 179, 180
Morocco 15-17, 64, 65, 66, 69-72, 75, 76, 80, 86, 89, 103, 115, 175, 177-179, 181
Mussolini, Benito 14, 17, 21, 22, 35, 37, 38, 48, 50, 54, 68, 70, 76, 78, 83, 84, 97, 101, 105, 109-111, 113, 118, 121, 123, 126-128, 148, 155-157, 162, 167, 168, 178-182, 187, 194, 195, 199

Negrín, López, Juan 126, 133-135, 138, 140, 152, 159
Nehru, Jawaharlal 124
Nin I Pérez, Andreu 133, 135

Orwell, George 56, 85, 135

Packenham-Walsh, Brigadier 77
Pact of San Sebastián 25, 32
Paterson, Harold 82
PCE (Partido Comunista Español) 55, 57, 58, 60, 81, 132
Pollard, Diana 68-71
Pollard, Hugh 68-71, 76, 82
Popular Front 14, 54, 55, 57-61, 64, 65, 72, 74, 75, 81, 95, 102, 131, 132, 142
Portugal 26, 45, 65, 69, 70, 78, 86, 91, 92, 136, 167, 191, 192
POUM (Partido Obrero de Unificación Marxista) 55, 56, 80, 81, 85, 107, 126, 133-135, 140
Primo de Rivera, José Antonio 67, 68, 87, 95, 117
Primo de Rivera, Miguel 17, 18, 20, 21, 27, 52, 67
PSOE (Partido, Socialista Obrero Español) 29, 31, 44, 54, 55, 57, 58, 60, 133

Puente Bahamonde, Ricardo de la (Major) 89, 90

Quiepo de Llano, Gonzalo (General) 71
Quiroga - see Casares Quiroga

Radical Republican Party (Partido Republicano Radical) 31, 44-46, 52-54, 57, 60
Republican Action Party (Acción Republicana) 33
Republican Left Party (Izquierda Republicana) 57, 58, 60
Republican Union (Unión Republicana) 58, 60
Romilly, Esmond 89, 92-94, 143, 144
Roosevelt, Franklin D 162, 173, 175, 189, 192, 197, 198

Salazar Alonso, Rafael 45
Salazar, António de Oliveira 136
Samper Ibáñez, Ricardo 45
Sanjurjo y Sacanell, José 27, 39-41, 65-67, 69, 70, 86, 100, 101, 117
Scottish Ambulance Unit 79
Soviet Union/Russia 13, 14, 39, 55, 74, 80-82, 102, 104, 105, 110, 112, 126, 131-140, 142, 143, 147, 149, 157, 170-173, 182-185, 188, 192, 198,
Suñer, Serrano 89, 92, 95-97, 171, 172, 174, 175, 177, 178, 181, 183, 185
Stalin, Joseph 81, 131, 132, 137, 142, 172

Tonypandy 9,10
Trotsky, Leon 55, 80, 81

UGT (Unión General de Trabajadores) 45, 55
USA 13, 22, 34, 37, 94, 146-148, 150, 170-175, 185, 189, 190, 192, 194-198, 200, 201
USC (Unió Socialista de Catalunya) 58

Watson, Dorothy 68-71

Yague, Juan 167-169